Developing Good Morals

God's Way vs. Satan's Way

Thank you for coming to VBS 2023 Woodstock

Enjoy your gifts
Ms C. Walton

Darryl Barron

Acknowledgments

All thanks and praise be to God for giving me the talent to write this book. Thanks to the following individuals: Wannetter Terrell Director of Gresham Park Recreation Center for allowing me the opportunity to volunteer during the afterschool program, which inspired me to find creative ways of introducing good morals to children, which in turn inspired me to write this book. I would also like to thank Rachel Barron, Aderyl Barron, Derryl Barron, Christopher Williams, Elizabeth Azeez, Jackson Bowen, Joshua Bryant, Vosco D. Williams, and John Samuel Snow.

Additionally, I would like to thank Elvira Weekes for her pivotal cover suggestion, Traci with an Eye for bringing reality to my drawing for the cover of this book, and Emmanuel Azeez for making adjustments to improve the cover.

Contents

Section 2

Introduction

I was inspired to write this workbook after volunteering at an afterschool program where I interacted with and read to children of various ages. I noticed the need for children to learn and develop good morals.

As I go about my everyday life, I observe and experience racial division, discourteous drivers, rudeness, inconsideration, insensitivity, and violence. I noticed the lack of morals in social media and news media, which made me realize that learning and developing good morals is an absolute need for everyone.

Therefore, I wrote this book to plant the seeds of good morals into your spirit to help you become more conscious of your actions. This book gives you a heads up on what is right and wrong and the consequences of the choices you make should you become influenced by your peers, tv, and social media.

This book contains over one hundred good and bad moral topics. Each topic has a relating poem, a scripture, a paragraph containing information important to know, and a true story example, followed by questions to engage the reader.

Just Reading

One or Two Pages a Day

Will Help You Develop

Good Morals God's Way

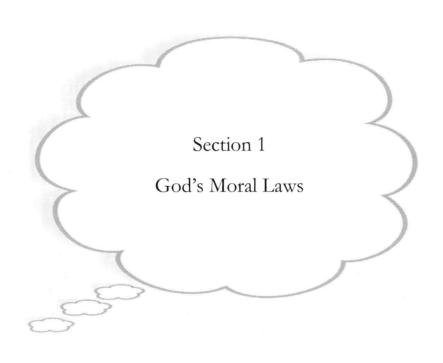

Section 1

God's Moral Laws

Morals

Morals are values, principles, and standards of behavior you live by that relate to right and wrong, good and bad, acceptable and unacceptable in society. Your moral values determine the quality of your character, how you choose to conduct yourself in society, and the eyes of God.

To have moral values is God's way.

To have immoral values is Satan's way (the devil).

God's way is doing what is good and right.

Satan's way is doing what is bad and wrong.

Some moral values are: loving others, being just, fair, honest, obedient, respectful, kind, helpful, sharing, and saying "thank you." <u>These moral values favor God because they are good and right.</u>

Some immoral values are: being unjust, hating others, selfish, unfair, disobedient, uncaring, rude, racist, mean, dishonest, disrespectful, and cruel. <u>These immoral values favor Satan because they are bad and wrong.</u>

Write one or two moral values you like that favor God.

Example: Loving others, _____

Write one or two immoral values you should avoid that favor Satan.

Example: Hating others, _____

What is good and right in many ways is moral. What is bad and wrong in many ways is immoral. It is Godly to be moral and ungodly to be immoral. In the Bible, **Deuteronomy 30:19 NIV** _"I have set before you, life and death, blessings and curses. Now choose life..."_ When God said, _"I set before you, life and death, blessings and curses,"_ He was giving people the free will, a choice to keep his word and obey or not.

Example: You have the choice of being obedient to God's word loving others, doing good and right, or being disobedient to God's word hating others, doing bad and wrong.

Deuteronomy Chapter 28 Moses indicates the blessings for obedience and curses for disobedience.

Death and curses started when the **serpent** convinced Eve to eat a fruit forbidden by God to eat. When Eve ate the forbidden fruit, she gave it to Adam, and he ate it. God cursed the **serpent** for convincing Eve to eat the forbidden fruit by causing it to crawl on its belly all the days of its life.

When Eve and Adam went against God by choosing to disobey Him (sin), they had a consequence to face, death (dying) and going back to the dust of the earth.

Genesis Chapter 3 tells the story of Adam and Eve.

Eve and Adam had to face the consequences of doing wrong. True__ False__

The serpent did. Good and right__ Bad and wrong __

Why did God curse the serpent? _____

_____

God's love, Goodness, and Righteousness Are the Foundation of Good Morals.

I John 4:16 ICB "*Whoever lives in love lives in God, and God lives in him.*"

Living a good moral life loving others, doing good and right shows that you have the love of God in your heart.

Good morals begin with love, the love of God. Love everyone, but love God first. Recognize that God is God, the creative force of the universe. God is love, and He made love a moral law, a law he wants everyone to abide by.

John 13:34 NIV "*Love one another. As I have loved you,*" To obey God's law of love is to love one another as God's word commands. When you love one another, you won't hate one another.

Proverbs 12:10 GNT "*Good people take care of their animals, but wicked people are cruel to theirs.*" You should show your love for God by loving Him and everything he created, including yourself, others, and animals.

What do good morals begin with? Love__ Hate__

Since animals are not people, you should not love them. True__ False__

Highlight in yellow the good moral words that favor God's way and circle in red the immoral words that favor Satan's way.

Love, hate, giving, taking, fighting, cursing, kindness, caring, lying, cheating, sharing, obedience, disobedient, disrespect, cruelty, respect, thank you, bullying, violence, stealing, friendly, being mean, uncaring, kill, violence, friendly, courteous, cursing.

Challenge:

Think of one or more words that favor God's way and write them on the line below.

Example: Helping,

_____

Think of one or more words that favor Satan's way.

Example: Violence,

_____

Choice: Place a checkmark on the way you choose to live.

God's way __

Satan's way (the devil) __

God's Creation of Laws

Genesis 1:1 KJV *"In the beginning, God created the heaven and earth."*
Genesis 1:25 KJV *"God made everything that creepeth upon the earth after his kind: and so, it was."*

Colossians 1:16 KJV *"For by him were all things created."* God created the earth, universe, planets, stars, moon, and sun.

God created laws such as the Law of Love, Moral Laws, the Law of Gravity, the Laws of Nature, the Law of Sowing and Reaping, the Ten Commandment Laws, and more.

God created laws so that people, animals, insects, and nature would have order, peace, and balance. Because of God's laws, everyone can abide on earth and enjoy the power and beauty of His creation in love, peace, and harmony.

Is God the creator of everything? Yes__   No__

God is not the first to create laws. True__   False__

Write one or more laws from the above paragraph that God created.
Example: God created the Law of Love.

_____

_____

God's Moral Laws

God is a moral god of love, goodness, and kindness. When God created heaven and earth, He created moral laws for everyone to obey and live by. Because God made obeying morals a law, it is right and good to love, wrong and bad to hate, right and good to give, wrong and bad to take, right and good to make peace and friends, wrong and bad to break the peace and pick fights, right and good to be honest, wrong, and bad to lie.

Mathew 25:46 BSB *"And they will go away into eternal punishment, but the righteous into eternal life."*

God is a righteous God, and because God is a righteous God, everyone who is righteous and obeys his laws will have eternal life, which is to live forever after death in God's heavenly presence.

Did God make obeying morals a law? Yes __ No__

Write one moral deed from the above paragraph that is right and good to do.

Example: It is right and good to give.

_____

Write one immoral deed from the above paragraph that is wrong and bad to do. **Example:** It is wrong and bad to take.

_____

God Is a righteous God? True __ False __

God is righteous means: God is a moral God__ God is an immoral God__

God's Law of Gravity

Psalm 104:5 NIV *"He set the earth on its foundations it can never be moved."*

Gravity is a physical law, a force that draws people and everything that has weight (mass) to the ground. Without gravity, you would float away like a balloon into the sky. The force of gravity makes an object drop to the ground when you throw it into the air. If you ignore the force of gravity and jump out of a window, <u>you will suffer the consequences</u> of dropping down (falling) to the ground fast and hard.

Although gravity has a scientific reason (explanation) for its existence, God is behind that reason because he is the creator of everything. Although the law of gravity has nothing to do with moral laws, the law of gravity and moral laws have two things in common. (1) God created both <u>moral laws</u> and the <u>law of gravity.</u> (2) Both laws <u>bear consequences.</u>

Example:

Steve and Jake wanted to test the force of gravity. They began throwing rubber balls into the air and watching them hit the ground. Jake became bored and wanted to try the law of gravity differently. He suggests jumping from a tree. But Steve refused because his mother told him not to jump from trees. Steve also knew that jumping from trees goes against the law of gravity and bears the consequence of hitting the ground hard.

God is not the creator of gravity. True___ False___

How many things does gravity have in common with moral laws? One___
Two___ Three___

God's Creation of Nature

Psalm 19:1 NIV *"The heavens declare the glory of God; the skies proclaim the work of his hands."*

Nature is everything outside that man did not make. Nature includes the fish in the sea, animals, bugs, grassy grounds, flowers, flying birds, and tall trees with leaves dangling down. Nature is the sun, the moon that lights the sky, and the twinkling stars among the galaxies up high. Nature is mountains, rain, sleet, and snow. Erupting volcanoes, blowing winds, and rivers that flow. The flashing of lightning and thunder that roars. Nature is all those things and so much more.

Although nature has a scientific reason (explanation) for its existence and order in which it operates, God is behind that reason and order because he is the creator of nature.

What do you like about God's creation of nature? **Example:** I like the falling leaves.

_____

_____

The Way Nature Obeys God's Laws

Psalm 147:8 KJV *"Who covereth the heavens with clouds, who prepareth rain for the earth, who maketh grass to grow upon the mountains."*

God created the laws of nature, which are natural actions of the earth and universe such as: How the sunlight and moonlight function and operate with an order. **Example:** When the sun rises in the morning, it obeys God's laws of nature to rise. When the moon and stars shine at night, they obey. When the rain falls from the sky, it obeys. When the wind blows, it also obeys God's laws of nature in the order it should.

Nature obeys God's law of order when flowers bloom with fragrance in the spring, when the sun shines hotter during summer, when leaves change colors and fall from the trees during autumn, when snow blankets the grounds, and cold rules the winter. God's laws of nature obeys by giving fish the ability to breathe underwater, birds' ability to fly, bugs' and animals' ability to feed themselves and take care of their young.

It is natural for God's laws of nature to function the way God created them to function. It is man's responsibility to respect the power of God's laws of nature or suffer the consequences.

Birds feeding their young is not a part of God's laws of nature. True___

False ___

When the wind blows, it's obeying God's laws of nature. True___

 False___

When the sun rises, it's not obeying God's laws of nature. True ___
False___

Weather is a part of God's laws of nature. True ___   False ___

Does spring, summer, fall, and winter function by God's laws of nature?

Yes ___   No ___

Example of Consequences for Not Respecting God's Laws of Nature

Job 37:6 NLT _"He directs the snow to fall on the earth and tells the rain to pour down."_

Animals such as bears respect the power of God's laws of nature by going into a deep sleep during the winter. If bears don't respect the power of cold weather, they would have difficulty finding enough food to survive and could die. If bugs don't respect the power of cold weather by finding warm places to stay during winter, they could die.

If you go outside when it is raining very hard, you will get wet; or drown in flood water for not respecting the power of heavy rain. If you stay outside when it is freezing cold, you could freeze to death. If you stay out in the hot sun too long, you could get sunburned or suffer a heat stroke. If you don't find a safe place during a tornado, you could be seriously injured or worse. If you are outside when it is lighting, you could be struck by lightning for not respecting the danger of lightning through the power of God's law of nature. Think about it for a moment. Being that animals and bugs obey and respect God's laws, so can you.

Are there consequences for not respecting the power of nature? Yes__ No__

Name one or more consequences you could face if you don't respect the power of God's laws of nature.

Example: You could freeze to death if you stay outside when it is freezing cold.

_____

_____

Review

Now you know that God is the creator of everything, and He God created laws that must obey. God's final creation was man (people).

Genesis 1:26 NASB "_Let Us make man in Our image, according to Our likeness._" God created (man-people) in his image and likeness. God's image and likeness includes his love for everyone, goodness, and moral nature. When you love others, have goodness in your heart for others, and have moral nature, you reflect the image and likeness of God.

When you hate others rather than love others, are selfish and unfair towards others rather than having goodness in your heart for them, immoral rather than moral, you do not reflect the image and likeness of God, but rather, the image and likeness of **Satan (the devil)**.

Although God wants you to live a moral life, He gives you the free will to make your own choices. Every moral and immoral choice you make, whether good or bad, will have consequences.

God has a moral nature. True__   False__

Satan has a moral nature. Ture__   False __

Sowing and Reaping

Galatians 6:7 KJV *"Be not deceived; God is not mocked for whatever a man soweth, that shall he also reap."*

Sowing and reaping is another law created by God. A law that causes you to have consequences sooner or later for your moral and immoral actions, deeds, and choices you make.

What you **sow-do** is like (planting a good-moral seed) or (a bad-immoral seed) through your actions, deeds, and choices you make.

What you **reap** are the consequences of what grows from **what you did,** which are those good-moral seeds or bad-immoral seeds you planted through your actions, deeds, and choices you made.

When you do something good, you will reap good by receiving or experiencing good in your life as a consequence of your good-moral action, deed, or choice you made. **When you do something bad,** you will reap bad by receiving or experiencing bad in your life as a consequence of your bad-immoral action, deed, or choice you made. Some people call those consequences "karma," but the truth is, you are reaping what you sowed because of God's law of sowing and reaping. Although karma is not in the bible, sowing and reaping are. But to many people sowing and reaping mean the same as karma.

God created the law of sowing and reaping. True__ False__

Your choices in everyday life determine if you reap good consequences or bad consequences. True __ False __

Example of Sowing and Reaping in a Good Way

One day Mary didn't bring her lunch to school, so her friend Daisy shared her lunch. Two days later, Daisy entered a contest and won a laptop. Daisy sowed a good deed seed when she shared her lunch with Mary and reaped good when she won the laptop.

Daisy reaped good consequences because she sowed (did) something good.

True__   False__

Who didn't bring their lunch to school?

_____

Example of Sowing and Reaping in a Bad Way

Sam stole Marcus's bookbag and said, "I didn't do it." Three months later, Sam's cellphone was stolen. Sam sowed (did) a bad thing when he stole Marcus's bookbag and eventually reaped bad when his cellphone was stolen.

What did Sam steal? _____

Sam reaped bad consequences because he did something bad. True__ False__

Remember, doing right and good means you are (sowing good), and when you sow good sooner or later, you will (reap good consequences).

Doing wrong and bad means you are (sowing bad), and when you sow bad sooner or later, you will (reap bad consequences). That's the bottom line.

Example of Emotional Sowing and Reaping in a Bad Way

It is not against the law to laugh; in fact, it is natural to laugh. Laughing is not against school rules unless, of course, you laugh out loud in a way that will disrupt the class; otherwise, laughing is simply laughing and will not get you into trouble. Laughing becomes a bad moral when you laugh at someone knowing that it makes them feel bad or hurt their feelings.

When you laugh at someone and don't care if it makes them feel bad or hurts their feelings, you will likely reap what you sow in the same way or in a different way in the future.

If you intentionally make someone feel bad or hurt their feelings, you will not likely reap what you sow in the future. True ___   False ___

Making someone feel bad on purpose is a good moral deed. True___ False___

How God's Moral Laws Fit into Your Everyday Life

Romans 2:6 NIV *"God will repay each person according to what they have done."* Morals fit into your everyday life through rules and laws you must follow at home, school, and in society. Rules you live by every day are based on good, bad, right, and wrong. This is proof that man's laws have good and bad principles in common with God's moral laws.

It is right to follow the rules and laws in the eyes of God and man. Whether your behavior is moral (good) or immoral (bad), God recognizes it and rewards you accordingly. Man also recognizes your behavior and rewards you accordingly.

It is not right to follow the rules and laws. True___ False___

God and man recognize your behavior, whether good (moral) or bad (immoral) and reward you accordingly. True___ false___

Example of How God's Moral Laws Fit into Your Everyday Life

When you make a good choice by doing the right thing, you will stay out of trouble. When you make a bad choice by doing the wrong thing, you will get into trouble. It's that simple.

When your parents ask you to do something, the moral thing to do is obey. Making a choice not to obey will result in bad consequences. It is against your school's Code of Conduct for you to talk on a cell phone during class, fight, or bring a weapon to school. The moral thing to do is to obey and follow the rules. Making a choice not to obey or follow the rules will result in serious consequences.

You cannot simply walk up to someone, slap them, and expect to walk away without facing the consequences of your wrong deed. However, you can walk up and help someone without getting into trouble because helping is an acceptable good moral deed.

You cannot simply walk up and take something from someone without facing the consequences for your wrong deed because taking is a form of bullying and robbery and will not be tolerated. However, you can walk up and give someone something without getting into trouble because giving is an acceptable good moral deed.

When you are at home, school, or elsewhere in society, you do not have to maintain the moral discipline necessary to stay out of trouble. True __

False __

When you make a moral choice to do the right thing, you will stay out of trouble. True __ False __

How Morals Relates to Your Conscience

Romans 2:15 NIV *"They show that the requirements of the law are written on their hearts, their consciences also bearing witness and their thoughts sometimes accusing them and at other times even defending them."*

Your conscience is the part of your mind that alarms and gives you moral guidance by causing you to feel bad in the form of guilt for something you may have done wrong. When you do something against your moral principles and values, your conscience will cause you to feel guilty and think about what you have done.

It is good when your conscience bothers you and makes you feel guilty because it means you are aware of your wrongdoing. Your conscience allows you the opportunity to apologize, repent, and do what is good and right.

It is important to listen and respond to your conscience whenever you feel guilty. When you stop listening and responding to your conscience, it will become inactive (stop working). When your conscience stops working, you will not feel guilty when you do wrong. But rather, you will develop bad, immoral principles and values.

You will also begin to behave recklessly; and become heartless and insensitive towards others, which could get you into trouble and cause you to go against the love of God and his moral laws.

When you do wrong and feel guilty about it, you have the love of God in your heart because your moral conscience is working. When you do wrong and don't care, you lack the love of God in your heart, and your moral conscience is not working.

Example:

Two teens, Robert and Kyle, robbed a store. The following week they robbed another store, then another store. One day, as they were robbing a store, Robert accidentally shot a six-year-old kid buying candy. Both Robert and Kyle panicked and ran without taking any money. Two weeks later, Kyle turned himself in to the police.

When the police asked Kyle, "why did you turn yourself in?" Kyle answered, "I couldn't sleep; my conscience was bothering me. I felt bad and couldn't stop thinking about the little kid getting shot."

Robert didn't care about turning himself in to the police because his conscience had become inactive (stopped working). He not only continued robbing stores, but he also carjacked a mother at gunpoint with her baby strapped in a car seat. Robert tried to get away while the mother and her baby were still in the car. There was a short police chase before Robert crashed the car. Robert was arrested and taken to jail. All thanks are to God that neither the mother nor her baby was hurt.

Kyle did the right thing and turned himself in to the police because his conscience made him feel bad. True___ False___

Robert didn't care about turning himself in to the police because his conscience had stopped working. True___ False___

Psalm 5:10 ESV *"Make them bear their guilt, O God; let them fall by their own Counsels; because of their many transgressions cast them out, for they have rebelled against you."*

Let your conscience be your guide. Don't allow your conscience to become inactive; otherwise, your heart and attitude will grow cold, mean, and uncaring towards others. Remember, when you do wrong and feel guilty about it after you do it, that's your conscience letting you know what you did was wrong. You should repent and do right, or you could suffer consequences.

Revelation 3:19 ESV *"Those whom I love, I reprove and discipline, so be zealous and repent."* God would discipline you if you chose not to repent. Repenting is to regret your wrongdoing, think what is good, and do right.

How Morals Relates to Common Sense

Proverbs 8:5 CSB *"Learn to be shrewd, you who are inexperienced, develop common sense, you who are foolish."* To be shrewd is to use good judgment and make smart decisions. The way to make smart decisions is by using commonsense. Common sense is using good sound judgment and thinking of the consequences before you make a choice.

God's word says, *"develop common sense."* To develop common sense as God's word commands, you must practice discretion and use good judgment until it becomes a habit. Once it becomes a habit, common sense will begin to work automatically in your mind by causing you to think ahead and fear the possibility of consequences before you make a bad choice.

The more you practice using common sense, the more likely you will make smarter choices. When you stop using common sense, you will likely make bad choices without fear of consequences, when you lack fear that the wisdom common sense gives you to think twice and look ahead at all possibilities of trouble or danger before making choices. You will likely make choices that will lead to reckless behavior, dangerous and bad consequences.

Psalms 25:12 NASB *"Who is the person who fears the Lord? He will instruct him in the way he should choose."*

Although it is good to have courage, it is wise to respond to fear when something could lead to trouble or bad consequences. Are you using common sense when you choose to do something wrong or dangerous without fear of consequences? When you don't use common sense, there is always a possibility of getting into trouble, hurt, or possibly worse.

Fear is a necessary emotion that will help guide and keep you from making wrong or bad choices. Not heeding to the fear common sense gives you could likely result in bad consequences.

Proverbs 16:22 ESV *"Good sense is a foundation of life to him who has it, but the instruction of fools is folly."*

Common sense will let you know what choices are wise to fear and unnecessary to fear. God expects you to fear Him enough to be obedient to His laws. Using common sense is when you think things through, use sound judgment and heed certain fears to avoid making bad, foolish, or stupid choices. When you use commonsense before choosing, you will likely know beforehand what decision would be wise, foolish, or stupid.

Example:

Brandon, Austin, and Mario each purchased a fast new car. They wanted to see which car was the fastest, so they decided to race. Brandon backed out on the day of the race because he was afraid of getting a speeding ticket or into an accident. Austin and Mario went ahead with the race. During the race, Mario hit a pole and killed himself. Austin wrecked his car but survived. He was given a ticket for speeding and arrested for vehicular homicide because the death occurred due to the racing.

Did Austin and Mario use common sense? Yes __ No__

Did a degree of fear play a role in the common sense used by Brandon when he backed out of the race? Yes__ No__

Three Choices of Life (Wise, Foolish, or Stupid)

Highlight in Yellow the Choice You Will Always Try to Make. 1, 2, or 3

(1) A wise choice is a choice you make when you use common sense, which leads to good consequences.

(2) A foolish choice is a choice you make without using common sense and without the thought of possible consequences.

(3) A stupid choice is an unintelligent choice you make without using common sense, knowing the likelihood of facing bad consequences.

Making a foolish or stupid choice could cause trouble, pain, damage, or possibly ruin your life.

Example:

Patrick was daring Malek and Adrian to pull the school fire alarm. Malek and Adrian refused to pull the fire alarm because they feared the consequences of getting into trouble. So, Patrick decided to pull the alarm himself in front of Malek, Adrian, and other students.

After Patrick pulled the fire alarm, the school was evacuated. When Mr. Adger, the Principal, learned that Patrick was the same student who previously pulled the fire alarm twice before, he was appalled.

Patrick was arrested and later sent to an alternative school because of his bad choice.

Which choice did Patrick make? (1.) Wise__ (2) Foolish__ (3) Stupid__

GOD'S TEN COMMANDMENTS LAWS Exodus 20:1-17 KJV

Commandment number (I) as written in the bible. *"Thou shalt have no other gods before me."*

Commandment number (I) explained: You should never love anyone or anything more than you love God.

Commandment number (II) as written in the bible. "Thou shalt not make unto thee any graven image...."

Commandment number (II) explained: You should never make yourself a god for worshiping or praying. You should only worship and pray to God in heaven above.

Commandment number (III) as written in the bible. *"Thou shalt not take the name of the Lord thy God in vain."*

Commandment number (III) explained: You should always respect the name of God and never use God's name in a bad way.

Commandment number (IV) as written in the bible. *"Remember the Sabbath day, to keep it holy."*

Commandment number (IV) explained: You can keep the Sabbath day holy by knowing that God made it a special day for you to relax, praise, and worship him.

Commandment number (V) as written in the bible. *"Honor thy Father and thy Mother: that thy days may be long upon the land which the Lord thy God giveth thee."*

Commandment number (V) explained: God wants you always to respect and obey your parents.

Commandment number **(VI)** as written in the bible. *"Thou shalt not kill."*

Commandment number **(VI)** explained: You should never kill (murder) anyone for immoral reasons.

Commandment number **(VII)** as written in the bible. *"Thou shalt not commit adultery."*

Commandment number **(VII)** explained: Should you marry one day, you should be honest to your husband or wife, keep your promise to be faithful, and never cheat.

Commandment number **(VIII)** as written in the bible. *"Thou shalt not steal."*

Commandment number **(VIII)** explained: God wants you to love others and respect what belongs to them by not taking or stealing.

Commandment number **(IX)** as written in the bible. *"Thou shalt not bear false witness against thy neighbor."*

Commandment number **(IX)** explained: Your neighbors are other people. God does not want you to be dishonest or go around lying about other people to other people.

Commandment number **(X)** as written in the bible. *"Thou shalt not covet thy neighbor's house..."*

Commandment number **(X)** explained: God wants you to appreciate what you have and not want to have what belongs to someone else.

Does God expect you to obey his Commandments? Yes __   No__

Are you going to try to obey God's Ten commandments? Yes__   No__

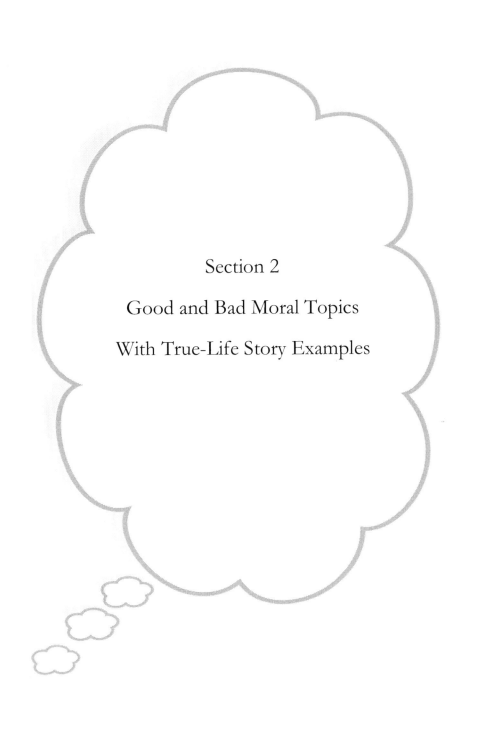

Section 2

Good and Bad Moral Topics

With True-Life Story Examples

Admit When You are Wrong

Admitting when you are wrong Start

Doesn't always necessarily feel good

But since admitting wrong is a good thing

Admitting wrong is something you always should.

Important to Know

I John 1:9 NIV *"If we confess our sins, he is faithful and just to forgive us or our sins and cleanse us from all unrighteousness."* Admitting when you are wrong can sometimes make you feel uncomfortable, embarrassed, and ashamed. Admitting you are wrong does not mean you are weak but instead shows you have the courage and integrity to face the truth and do the right thing.

Example:

Jaden and Amber's mother told them to take their rain jackets to school because it was going to rain. But since the skies were blue, they didn't believe it was going to rain, so they didn't take their rain jackets as they were told. Later that day, it did rain. Jaden and Amber got soaked and wet.

When their mother came home, they told her they got wet because they didn't take their jackets to school. They admitted they were wrong and apologized for disobeying her. Their mother appreciated the courage and integrity they showed by admitting they were wrong.

Admitting that you are wrong shows you have enough courage and integrity to face the truth and do the right thing. True __ False __

Jaden and Amber did well by admitting they were wrong. True __ False

Arrogance

No one is ever better or

Superior because he possesses

More than another for we are all

Created equal as sisters and brothers

Important to Know

Jeremiah 50:31 BSB _"Behold, I am against you, O arrogant one, declares the Lord God of Host."_ It is good to be proud of yourself. But you are arrogant when you allow your proud achievements and worldly possessions to cause you to look down on others or think you are better than others. No one is better than anyone else, no matter who they are or what they have because God created everyone equally. Whether you're rich, poor, or in between, remember **Ecclesiastes 3:20, 21 NIV** _"All go to the same place; all come from dust, and to dust all return."_ So, who's better? No one.

Example:

Barry and Sandra think they are better than others because they are popular, have lots of money, an expensive home, expensive cars, and more. They feel like people who don't have equal or more than what they have make them less than they are. When others speak (greet), Barry and Sandra turn their heads and are unfriendly.

Do you think Barry and Sandra are arrogant? Yes__ No__

No one is better than anyone else because God created everyone equally. True __ False __

Allow Someone Else to Be First Sometime

Allowing someone else to be first

Allowing someone else to go before you

Is a very kind and godly thing for you to do.

Important to Know

Philippians 2:3 NLT *"Don't be selfish; don't try to impress others. Be humble, thinking of others as better than yourselves."* God gave man the instinct that causes you to want to be first, stand out, and get the most attention. Dr. Martin Luther King Jr. called it "The Drum Major Instinct." Although the instinct to be first is natural, God did not intend for man to behave being first for personal or selfish reasons. God gave man such an instinct to behave by being first to love, first to give, first to help, first to forgive, first to be courteous, first to be friendly, first to walk away from a fight, first to avoid wrong and do right. God wants you to stand out and be the first to get attention in a positive way, not in a negative or selfish way.

Example:

Danny was on crutches while waiting for the school bus, along with several other students. When the bus arrived, the other students allowed Danny to enter first. When Danny's leg got better, he began allowing fellow students to enter the school bus and building first. Now, almost all the students allow each other to be first and feel good about it.

God wants you to be first in a positive way. True __ False __

Is it good to allow someone else to be first? True__ False__

Attitude

A bad attitude is not best

A bad attitude causes much stress

A bad attitude is often mean and cold

A bad attitude is something you can control

Important to Know

Ephesians 4:31 KJV *"Let all bitterness, and wrath, and anger, and clamour, and evil speaking, be put away from you, with all malice."* A bad attitude is negative, selfish, uncooperative, unfriendly, and mean. You must be positive, kind, friendly, considerate, and understanding to have a good attitude. No one wants to be around a person with a bad attitude. But most everyone likes being around people with a good attitude.

Example:

Jan, Alia, and Sophia attended a sleepover at the home of Kathy, a popular student. They ate pizza, popcorn, drank sodas, and enjoyed a movie. Alia had a deck of Uno cards. While they were playing, Alia became angry because she couldn't win and decided to take her Uno cards and go home.

Scott, Bryan, Lorenzo, and Seth were playing football. Seth got angry because he couldn't change the rules, so he quit playing.

Did Alia have a bad attitude? Yes__ No__

Circle the name of the boy who had a bad attitude. Scott, Bryan, Lorenzo, Seth.

Apologize

Apologize when you're sorry

Or whenever you make a mistake

It's always better to apologize right away

Because it gets harder to apologize when you wait.

Important to Know

James 5:16 KJV <u>"Confess your faults one to another,"</u> It is good to apologize. Apologizing doesn't always mean you're the person who's wrong or at fault. Apologizing makes peace, repairs friendship, and relationships. Apologizing also shows you care, paves the way for forgiveness, helps you and the person you are apologizing to feel better, and it makes you the bigger person.

Example:

Best friends Erica and Brittany are in the same classroom. One day Tyra, a classmate, began teasing Erica. To Erica's surprise, Brittany laughed each time Tyra teased her. When Brittany realized she was hurting her best friend Erica's feelings by laughing at her, her conscience made her feel bad so, to save their friendship, she stopped laughing and decided to apologize. Brittany's apology made Erica feel better, and they remained best friends.

Do you think Erica and Brittany would have remained best friends if Brittany had not apologized? Yes__   No__

Do you think that Brittany's conscience inspired her to apologize? Yes __ No__

Bad Conduct

It's wrong to be Bad

It's wrong for you to disobey

It's right to always do as you are told

And conduct yourself in a good moral way.

Important to Know

Philippians 1:27 NIV _"Whatever happens conduct yourselves in a manner worthy of the gospel of Christ."_ You might feel like you are in control when you are bad and breaking rules. But breaking the rules and bad conduct (behavior) will always lead to trouble. Whether you're breaking the rules in person or on social media for a few minutes of fame, bad conduct and breaking the rules will always have consequences.

Example:

   Nick and Quantavious were yelling, cursing, throwing things, and starting fights simply to make a video to post online during school. They did get their five minutes of fame as their video went viral. They also got suspended and a trip to jail. It made them realize that doing wrong for negative attention is not worth the trouble.

What was the consequences for the bad conduct of the Nick and Quantavious?

_____

_____

Was posting the video worth getting into trouble? Yes__ No__

Appreciation

It's good to show some appreciation

When someone does something nice for you

Making a habit of saying thank you or I appreciate it

Is a good habit to develop and a positive moral thing to do.

Important to Know

I Thessalonians 5:18 ESV *"Give thanks in all circumstances, for this is the will of God in Christ Jesus for you."* Expressing appreciation begins with giving thanks. When someone does something good for you, you should show appreciation. Saying thank you is one way of showing your appreciation. You can also show your appreciation with a hug or by doing something nice for someone. Showing appreciation is good, and it feels good to know when you're appreciated.

Example:

Ron and his sister Missy live in a comfortable home with their mother. Their mother works very hard every day to ensure that Ron and Missy have a roof over their heads, food to eat, clothes, shoes, school supplies, electronics, and more. One Saturday morning, Ron and Missy cleaned the house very well for their mother. They kissed her and said, "We appreciate everything you do for us."

Is it good to show appreciation? Yes___ No___

Do you think the appreciation Ron and Missy expressed to their mother made her feel good and happy? Yes___ No___

Being Cruel

It's cruel when you purposely

Hurt someone or cause them pain

Whether it be a person or an animal

All cruelty is a bad and ungodly shame.

Important to Know

Proverbs 11:17 KJV _"The merciful man does good to his own soul, but he who is cruel troubles his own flesh."_ When you intentionally cause someone harm or pain without mercy, you are being cruel. Hitting, hurting, yelling, teasing, laughing, bullying, and talking bad about others are all forms of cruelty. Being mean, abusive, and depriving an animal of its needs is also cruel.

Example:

Two students, Beatriz and Chelsy, were teasing Malissa, which made her sad. But Beatriz and Chelsy didn't care; they continued teasing Malissa. Malissa was so sad that she didn't want to go back to school anymore. Malissa's mother talked to the principal about Beatriz and Chelsy teasing Malissa. The principal warned them if they continued teasing her, they would be suspended.

Kalvin and David were walking home from school. Along the way, they saw a dog with an injured leg. Kalvin kicked the dog on his injured leg and laughed. David told Kalvin to stop, but he kicked the dog repeatedly.

Beatriz and Chelsy were cruel to Malissa. True__ False__

Circle the name of the person who was cruel to the dog. David Kalvin

Asking

Asking helps you obtain permission

Asking gives you what you need to know

Asking shows you're someone who has respect

Asking is how to obtain the knowledge to grow and grow.

Important to Know

Matthew 7:7 KJV *"Ask and it shall be given you; seek, and ye shall find; knock, and it shall be opened unto you:"* It is good and polite to ask. Asking increases knowledge and could keep you out of trouble, whereas not asking could get you into trouble. Asking makes you think, acknowledge, respect boundaries, and recognize authority. Asking also lets you know what you can and cannot do.

Example:

Samuel and Judy's mother were sick. They asked their pastor how they should pray for her to get better. The pastor said to them, *"pray by asking God to help your mother get better in Jesus's name and believe it.* Just as the pastor told them, Samuel and Judy prayed, and their mother got better. Now they know how to pray because they asked.

Richie walked out of the classroom. When he returned, the teacher asked him, "why did you walk out of the classroom?" Richie replied. "I had to use the restroom."

Highlight or circle what the pastor told Samuel and Judy to do.

Should Richie have asked for permission to use the restroom? Yes __

No __

Being Mean

It's not good to be mean

But rather it's nice to be kind

Being mean makes people avoid you

But being nice makes new friends all the time.

Important to Know

Ephesians 4:32 NIV *"Be kind and compassionate to one another,"* It's better to be helpful, kind, and friendly rather than be mean. Being mean makes you unfriendly and causes people not to like you. Being mean provokes other people to become mean too, and when everybody is mean, there is no one left to be kind and friendly.

Example:

Sisters, Missy and Journey, shared the same bedroom but different beds. Missy was always yelling at Journey when she asked her a question or sat on her bed. One night, Missy had a nightmare and asked Journey if she could sleep in her bed with her. Journey pulled back the covers and said, "sure." After that night, Missy was never mean to Journey again.

Mr. Edward had an apple tree in his backyard full of sweet apples. Patrick and his friends asked if they could pick some apples. Mr. Edward yelled, "no!" He then demands them to leave. One day Patrick saw Mr. Edward fall. He ran over and helped him up. Mr. Edward apologized for being mean and began allowing Patrick and his friends to pick apples from his tree.

Circle the name of the sister who was mean. Missy   Journey

Did Mr. Edward apologize for being mean? Yes__   No__

Being Fair

To be fair

Is to follow rules

And always do right

To be un-bios and equal

Towards others in God's sight.

Important to Know

Psalm 106:3 ESV *"Blessed are they who observe justice, who do righteousness at all times!"* Being fair is doing the right thing, being honest and truthful without cheating or showing favoritism. Being fair is not doing what you want or like, but what is true, reasonable, and right.

Example:

The teachers threw a party in the gymnasium for the students during school. They selected Tyra to serve sandwiches and Beth to serve the punch. The students began dancing and having fun. Later as they lined up for refreshments, April saw that her friend Beth was serving the punch so, she jumped the line and asked Beth to pour her punch first. Beth said, "I can't do that." "Why not?" Asked April. "Because it won't be fair to the other students who are waiting in line." Said Beth.

Which one of the girls was being fair? Beth__   April__

Write the name of the student who served the sandwiches.

_____

_____

Bullying

Bullying is a mean

And cruel thing to do

If know someone being bullied

Or should someone start bullying you

Report it because it's the right thing to do.

Important to Know

Psalm 138:7 CSB *"If I walk into the thick of danger, you will preserve my life from the anger of my enemies."* No one should accept being bullied. Bullying is threatening or forcing someone through harassing, verbal, written, or physical force to harm or frighten. Bullying, which includes cyberbullying, is a serious offense. Bullying causes people to want to harm themselves or retaliate with violence. How would you feel if someone bullies you, someone you love or care about?

Example:

Two students, Laura and Ciera, were bullying Angel during school. After school, they began Cyberbullying her. Angel was so terrified that her parents reported Laura and Ciera to the school principal and the police. Laura and Ciera were suspended from school and arrested when the police reviewed their threats on social media.

Cyberbullying cannot get you into trouble. True___ False___

Bullying is not serious. True___ False___

Being Humble

Being humble listens more

Instead of being the one that talks

It's backing down when others are agitated

Knowing when to yield and when to take a walk

Important to Know

Proverbs 15:1 ESV *"A soft answer turns away wrath, but a harsh word stirs up anger."* When you are modest, gentle, speak with kind words and tones, focus on the needs of others rather than your own, and don't mind being last, you're humble. Being humble does not mean you are weak or less than others, but rather, it shows you are understanding and have good moral values.

Example:

   Ron sat in Mike's assigned chair during class just to be rude. No problem, Mike simply sat in another chair. Ron said mean things to Mike and tried to argue with him, but Mike was too humble to argue back. He simply said, "I have no beef with you," and walked away.

   The next day Mike stood aside and allowed several students, including Ron, to enter the classroom first. Mike doesn't mind listening to people who disagree with him. He admits when he is wrong and is always calm when someone is yelling, angry, or hostile.

What is the name of the student who was trying to cause trouble?

Robert__   Ron__

Highlight or underline whatever you think is an act of Mike being humble.

Cheating

Though it's easy to cheat

Cheating is bad and wrong to do

It's a deed that's unfair and dishonest

And will cause distrust and problems for you.

Important to Know

Proverbs 11:3 NIV *"The integrity of the upright guides them, but the unfaithful are destroyed by their duplicity."* When you have good moral values, your conscience will lead you to do the right thing. Though sometimes it may be easy and convenient to cheat, it is just as easy and convenient not to cheat. You will not have to face any consequences when you don't cheat. But when you tend to cheat, eventually, you will get caught and must face the consequences.

Example:

Ms. Smith, a teacher, gave a test and asked the students not to get the answers from the internet. Two of the students, Pat, and Marcus got their answers from the internet anyway. When Ms. Smith learned that Pat and Marcus cheated on their test, she gave them a failing mark. She also lost trust in them, and that's bad when people cannot trust you.

It is okay to cheat just so you don't get caught. True___ False___

Underline what Pat and Marcus did wrong and circle the consequences of their actions.

Being Kind

Being kind is the right thing to do

So, be kind to all people and animals too.

Important to Know

Romans 12:10 KJV *"Be kindly affectioned one to another with brotherly love; in honor preferring one another;"* Being kind is to show love, be caring, helpful, friendly, and considerate of the needs of others. Being kind makes you feel good, and it is also contagious because when you are kind, others start being kind.

Example:

Noah, Tony, and Elizabeth were about to enter a store. An adult lady (elder) was behind them, waiting to enter. <u>Noah held the door open for the lady, allowing her to enter the store first.</u> The lady said, "thank you," and walked through. Although Noah didn't know it, his kind deed made the lady feel good.

What were Noah's two kind deeds?

_____

_____

Practice being kind and see what positive effects your kindness brings.

Cursing and Yelling

It's disrespectful to curse

It's rowdy when you opt to yell

Yelling is a form of disorderly conduct

A public behavior that could end you in jail.

Important to Know

Ephesians 4:29 ISV *"Let not filthy talk be heard from your mouths, but only what is good for building up people and meeting the need of the moment."* Cursing and yelling are bad forms of disorderly conduct. It shows you lack self-control, respect for others and yourself. It also shows you could care less about how disrespectful, violent, and indecent it makes you look.

Example:

Deja and Kim were yelling at each other across the classroom. When the teacher asked them to stop, Daja stopped, but Kim continued and got into trouble.

Brett and Devonte were yelling and cursing on the school bus. The bus driver reported their behavior to the principal. Brett and Devonte were suspended from riding the school bus for two weeks. Their parents were disappointed by their rude and disrespectful behavior. They were also angry because they had to find a way to get them to and from school for two weeks.

Cursing and yelling are disorderly and show you lack self-control. True__ False__

Brett and Devonte were suspended for bad behavior. True__   False__

Caring

Caring is a kindness and concern

That you have in your heart for others

With a Godly love as sisters and brothers.

Important to Know

Galatians 6:2 ESV *"Bear one another's burdens, and so fulfill the law of Christ."* It is good and godly to care for others. When you care, it matters to you how others feel, how they are doing, whether they are treated equally, good, bad, right, or wrong. He that care is not biased or selfish, but rather fair, considerate, and sensitive to others' wellbeing and needs.

Example:

Kyle, a new student sitting alone, seemed uncomfortable and sad because he did not know anyone. Best friends Zachary, and Lee cared enough to go over to Kyle, introduce themselves, and talk to him. It made him feel welcome and more comfortable.

Weston lost his lunch money. Carlos, a fellow student, cared enough to give him money to buy lunch. Weston appreciated Carlos for giving him the money. The next day Weston paid Carlos back the money he had given him, and they became good friends.

Which student felt uncomfortable and sad? _____

Carlos did not show care for Weston. True__ False__

Drinking Underage

Underage drinking is never cool

Underage drinking is breaking the rules

Underage drinking wrecks a beautiful mind

It causes bad decision making and trouble every time.

Important to Know

Proverbs 20:1 ESV *"Wine is a mocker, strong drink is a brawler, whosoever is led astray by it is not wise."* Underage drinking is against the law. It causes you to make bad decisions such as arguing, fighting, inappropriate touching, and driving under the influence. Underage drinking has the potentials to lead to injuries, jail, or worse. It also increases the risk of developing worse drinking problems or substance abuse later in life.

Example:

Austin, Justin, and Nicholas were talking and having fun after school. Austin and Justin started drinking and tried to get Nicholas to drink with them, but Nicholas chose not to drink. They tried taunting him but, Nickolas didn't allow it to influence his decision not to drink, which shows he is wise and in control of making his own decisions.

Is underage drinking against the law? Yes__ No__

Can underage drinking cause you to make bad decisions? Yes__ No__

Are you strong minded enough to make your own decisions or are you easily influences by other? Write your answer below.

_____

_____

Compassion

To have compassion is to be sensitive

To the misfortunes of others and animals too

With love and understanding as God have for you.

Important to Know

I Peter 3:8 NIV *"Finally, all of you, be like-minded, be sympathetic, love one another, be compassionate and humble."* Compassion is to have care and feelings for someone who may be feeling sad, hurting, needs help, or having a hard time. It is compassion that makes you feel sorry for someone, be kind, supportive, and concerned for others' feelings, needs, and sufferings, including animals.

Example:

During lunch, David tripped and fell on the cafeteria floor. Machelle, a fellow student, felt sorry for him and helped him up, making him feel better and less embarrassed.

Maria, a little girl, saw a frail stray cat walking through the neighborhood. She was concerned and told her mother about the cat. Her mother fed the cat and took care of it until animal control arrived. Now the cat is safe, no longer at risk of starving, and has a chance of being adopted.

Did Machelle show compassion for David after he fell?

Yes __ No __

Who showed compassion for the cat?

_____

Drugs

You should never use drugs

Neither should you sell drugs too

Using drugs is very bad for your health

Selling drugs is also bad and illegal to do.

Important to Know

Titus 2:11,12 NIV *"For the grace of God has appeared that offers salvation to all people. It teaches us to say "No" to ungodliness and worldly passions, and to live self-controlled, upright and godly lives..."* Using drugs is addictive and causes severe and sometimes irreversible health problems. People have been known to lose their minds after using drugs. Selling drugs is just as bad as using drugs because both could cause you to get hurt, killed, or sent to jail. Drugs are bad news whether you use them or sell them because either way, drugs lead to a dead end.

Example:

Tony and Richard were selling and using drugs and asked Steven to join them, but he refused. They dared him, but he didn't fall for it. A month later, Richard sold drugs to an undercover police officer and went to jail. Tony's drug use caused him to lose his mind.

Circle the name of the boys who used drugs. Steven   Richard   Tony

Drugs do not cause trouble. True__   False__

Compliment

Compliment someone

It will certainly make their day

Say something very nice about them

That you notice as you go about your way.

Important to Know

Proverbs 16:24 NASB *"Pleasant words are a honeycomb, sweet to the soul and healing to the bones."* It's nice to compliment people. You may compliment someone's smile, voice, eyes, hair, shoes, clothes, or accomplishments. People like compliments. Anything you like about someone deserves a compliment. Compliments make people feel good about themselves and create a positive atmosphere.

Example:

On the first day of school, Macy told Amber, "Her hair looks nice." Amber said, "thank you." Macy's compliment made Amber feel good about herself for the rest of the day.

Theo and Cody were sitting next to each other in class. Cody had a fresh haircut. Theo told Cody, "His haircut looks cool." Cody said, "thanks, I like your tennis shoes."

It is not nice when you compliment people. True __ False __

Observe someone, see what you like about them, and compliment them.

Fighting

Violence never solves anything

Therefore, it's useless for you to fight

There are much better ways of solving issues

It's wiser to walk away because fighting isn't right.

Important to Know

Titus 3:2 KJV _"Speak evil of no man, to be no brawlers, but gentle, showing all meekness unto all men."_ Fighting never solves anything, but rather, it makes matters worse. Fighting is violent and could lead to trouble, more violence, serious injuries, jail, and sometimes death. Fighting sometimes affects your family, friends, and others in an emotional and disruptive manner. Fighting is trouble you can avoid by recognizing when to keep quiet and when to walk away.

Example:

Two students, Mark and Ronald, were arguing. Ronald became angry and began yelling and cursing. Mark knew that yelling and cursing was a sign of anger and hostility that could lead to fighting so, he stopped arguing and said to Ronald, "Okay, you got it" and walked away.

Fighting could lead to trouble and make matters worse. True ___ False ___

What can you do to avoid a fight?

_____

_____

Considerate

To be considerate

Is to be unselfish and fair

To care about how others feel

And have the heart to show some care.

Important to Know

Philippians 2:4 ESV *"Let each of you look not only to his own interest but also to the interest of others."* Being considerate is when you compromise, are helpful, nice, caring, fair, patient, kind, and respectful of others. Being considerate is also when you think of the needs and feelings of others rather than your own.

Example:

Twins, Mack and Zack, wanted their mother to buy a pizza, but she didn't have the money. Zack became angry and developed an attitude. Mack understood and didn't get angry.

Is it easy or hard to be considerate of others? Easy__ Hard__

Which twin was not considerate, and why?

_____

_____

Forcing

Never try to force anyone

To do what they don't want to do

It will cause you to get into much trouble

The kind that sends police to seek and arrest you.

Important to Know

Matthew 7:12 ESV *"So whatever you wish that others would do to you, do also to them, for this is the Law and the Prophets."* Forcing is a form of bullying that is controlling and disrespectful. Anytime you force someone to do something against their will, you are not just hurting their mind; you are also committing a crime. If someone tries to force you to do something you don't want to do in any way, you should report it right away.

Example:

Jody forced Amaya to hug and kiss him during school. Amaya told the principal. Jody was suspended from school and sent to juvenile for sexual assault. Now he has a criminal record that will follow him for the rest of his life.

A group of students was riding the school bus. When the bus stopped, Mia forced Aaliyah to stay in her seat. The bus driver reported the incident to the proper authority, and Mia was suspended from riding the school bus for a month.

Is forcing someone a serious offense? Yes __   No __

How would you feel if someone forced you to do something you do not want to do? Good__   Bad__

Courteous

Be polite to others

Have a positive attitude

Make an effort to be kind

Have respect and don't be rude.

Important to Know

I Peter 3:8 NASB *"To sum it up, all of you be harmonious, sympathetic, brotherly, kindhearted and humble in spirit."* It is easy to be courteous. Being courteous is when you are kind, friendly, and polite. When you say "thank you" or greet someone by saying "hi, hey, or hello." Being courteous is also when you offer your seat to allow someone else to sit down, allow someone else to be first, or hold the door open for someone. Being courteous is an excellent moral quality have.

Example:

A group of seven students entered the school building. One of the seven students, Joseph held the door open and allowed the other six to enter first. Three of the six students appreciated his courtesy and expressed it by saying "thank you." The other three said nothing.

What are the two good morals of this story? Hint-underlined.

_____
_____
_____

Think of what you can do to be courteous and do it.

Gangs

Gangs are violent and not for you

They're always hurting and killing each other

Creating trouble and violence is what gangs often do.

Important to Know

Proverbs 13:20 NIV *"Walk with the wise and become wise, for a companion of fools suffers harm."* It is not good to join a gang. Gangs are controlling, violent, always breaking laws, rules, and telling you bad things to do. They are also known for robbing or getting robbed, hurting or getting hurt, and killing or getting killed. Gang members go to jail for their crimes, and if you join a gang, these things could happen to you.

Example:

Scott was a straight-A student who received several honors. One day Scott joined a gang and robbed a store with Drew, a fellow gang member. In the process, the store owner was shot and killed. Drew was sentenced to life in prison for robbing and killing the store owner. Even though Scott didn't kill the store owner himself, he was also sentenced to life in prison for participating.

Sisters Margaret and Marsha joined a gang. The gang leader told the sisters to rob their mother. When Margaret and Marsha refused, they were beaten by fellow gang members.

Gangs will force you to do what they tell you to do. True__   False__

Gangs are not violent. True__   False__

Do unto Others

The golden rule is to

Always do unto others

As you would have others

Respect you and do unto you.

Important to Know

Luke 6:31 NIV *"Do unto others as you would have them do to you."* You should treat others the way you want to be treated. This is God's way for you to maintain love and respect for one another. You should not do or say anything to anyone in a way you wouldn't want to be done or said to you. You should treat others with kindness, consideration, and respect, knowing that you would like to be treated the same.

Example:

Sisters, Keosha and Marsha had new iPads. Marsha dropped her iPad on the floor and cracked the screen. She took Keosha's iPad without her permission and accidentally cracked the screen on it too.

Do you think Marsha would like it if Keosha took something that belonged to her without her permission? Yes ___ No ___

Was it respectful of Marsha to use Keosha's iPad without her permission? Yes___ No___

Greed

When you try to get

More than you'll ever need

You have developed in your heart

A greedy and selfish desire called greed.

Important to Know

Luke 12:15 NIV _"Watch out! Be on your guard against all kinds of greed; life does not consist in an abundance of possessions."_ Greed is when you allow your greediness to get the best of you. You can have greed for control, money, food, or anything. When you have greed in your heart, you are never satisfied and take every opportunity to get more and more of what you don't necessarily need.

Example:

Joey and Mario each were given free all-you-can-eat Krispy Kreme doughnuts for dining. Both Joey and Mario ate seven doughnuts each and became full. Mario decided not to eat any more doughnuts. Joey decided to eat ten more and developed a severe stomachache being greedy.

Danny works at Wendy's. His neighbor, Chrissy, paid him seventy-five dollars for cutting her grass. She asked Danny to bring his brother Chance the next time, but he didn't. Danny cut their grass all summer without telling Chance anything because he wanted to make all the money for himself.

Which student had greed? Mario__   Joey__

Which brother had greed? Danny__   Chance__

Following Rules

It's good to follow rules

It's very wise for you to obey

Following rules keep you inline

And keep you out of trouble each day.

Important to Know

Hebrews 13:17 KJV *"Obey them that have rule over you and submit yourselves:"* Rules are made for a reason. When everyone follows the rules, everything stays in order, and everyone stays out of trouble. All it takes is one individual to break a rule to create trouble for themselves and others. When rules are broken, trouble and consequences will follow.

Example:

Janice was using her cellphone during class, which violates the school rules. Her teacher Ms. Brooks took her cell phone, and her parents had to come to the school to retrieve it. On that same day, Deigo brought a gun to school. He was arrested, transported to juvenile, and was never seen in a school setting again.

Did Janice and Diego get into trouble for not following the rules? Yes __ No _

When you break a rule there are no consequences. True__ False__

Grudge

When you feel bitter angry and quite unfriendly

For something that happened in the past

Unforgiving and refuse to budge

You are holding in your heart

An ungodly grudge.

Important to Know

Colossians 3:8 NLT *"But, now is the time to get rid of anger, rage, malicious behavior, slander, and dirty language."* Holding a grudge is when you continue to feel angry and bitter about something that happened in the past. Holding a grudge could cause you to develop hate in your heart, feel negative, angry, mean, and unforgiving. It could also spoil your peace of mind, and when your mind is not at peace, it's hard to be happy.

Example:

During school, Shawanda slapped Monica in her face and denied it. Emmanuel saw her do it and told the principal the truth about what he saw, which caused Shawanda to get arrested for assault. Two years later, Shawanda was still angry and bitter at Emmanuel even though she knew she did wrong when she slapped Monica.

Was Shawanda holding a grudge two years later? Yes__ No__

The above scripture says, "get rid of anger, rage and malicious behavior. True__ False__

Forgive

God forgives us

When we forgive others

So let's try to be more God-like

And be more forgiving of each other.

Important to Know

Matthew 6:14,15 KJV *"For if you forgive men their trespasses, your heavenly Father will also forgive you, but if you forgive not men their trespasses, neither will your Father forgive your trespasses."* God wants you to be forgiving of others, for He forgives you. It is good to forgive rather than allow the bitterness of unforgiveness to anger you and break the peace in your mind and heart. Forgiving does not mean you must forget, but rather it helps you to let go, move forward and be at peace with yourself and the person you forgive.

Example:

   Siblings, Zosar and Malik, had their friend Mark visit. Mark broke a lamp and told their mother Zosar and Malik broke the lamp, which caused them to be punished. A week later, Mark apologized to the siblings and told [their mother the truth. Zosar forgave Mark and they continued to have fun together. Malik refused to forgive Mark. Instead, he remained angry and bitter.

Which sibling do you think is happier? Zosar__ Malik__

If you forgive others, God will forgive you. True__ False__

Guns and Knives

Handling either a gun or knife

Should never ever be something fun

Should either be brandished it's time to run

Important to Know

Ecclesiastes 9:18 NIV *"Wisdom is better than weapons of war, but one sinner destroys much good."* Guns and knives are dangerous and nothing to play with. Many people have been accidentally shot and killed playing with guns or injured playing with knives. You should never bring a gun or knife to school. If you are caught with a gun or knife, you could be arrested and taken to jail.

Example:

Two friends, Keith and Stanton, were playing a video game. Keith took out a sharp pocketknife. He asked Stanton if he thought he was fast enough to snatch the knife out of his hand with the blade open. Stanton said, "yes." Stanton failed to grab the knife on his first attempt. However, he succeeded in cutting his fingers to the bone on his second attempt.

After school, Paul found a loaded handgun lying on his father's dresser and decided to take a selfie with it. When he picked up the gun, it fired a shot shattering the mirror. The loud bang startled Paul, causing him to drop the gun. When he dropped the gun, it fired another shot grazing his head.

Was it safe for Keith and Stanton to play with a knife? Yes__   No__

When Paul picked up his father's gun, he could have accidentally killed himself. True__   False__

Giving

It's better to give

Than it is to receive

When you give to others

You come to bless their needs.

Important to Know

Luke 6:38 NIV *"Give, and it shall be given to you."* **Acts 20:35 NIV** *"It's more blessed to give than to receive."* When you give, you should give from your heart without expecting anything in return. It is good to give. Giving makes you feel good and others happy. You don't always have to give money. You can give your time, help, kind words, gifts, or anything someone may need or like. Giving shows, you are kind, friendly, and have love and care in your heart for others.

Example:

Two friends, Wong and Dion, went on a field trip with their class. When it was time to eat lunch, they noticed Paul, a fellow student, had only a sandwich for his lunch. Wong gave Paul some cookies, Dion gave him a soda. Because Wong and Dion chose to give, they made someone happy.

Giving money is the only way to give. True__ False__

When you give you should not expect anything in return. True__ False__

Hate

Hating someone is the opposite of love

It is wrong to hate each other said God above

He that has hate in his heart cannot love or forgive

And wherever there is hate the love of God cannot reveal.

Important to Know

Proverbs 8:13 KJV *"The fear of the Lord is to hate evil:"* Hating is bad unless you hate what God hates. God hates evil. Evil is contrary to God's moral nature of love. Therefore, it is wrong to hate others. Hating others poisons your mind making you open to bad and evil thoughts. Hating others also causes you to be mean, unkind and develop unnecessary anger and bitterness in your heart.

Example:

A group of students hated to see people of different races together as friends. Every day during lunch, they would move away if friends of other races sat close to them. But that did not bother the mixed-race friends because they have love and happiness in their hearts for people rather than hate and anger.

Two students, Lee and Joseph, were beaten in a school stairway by three other students because of their race. The beating was investigated and deemed a hate crime. The students involved in the beating were arrested, sent to jail, and charged with a serious hate crime.

Hating people is wrong. True__   False__

It is okay to hate someone if they are of a different race. True__   False__

Good is Good

Doing right and being good

Is very much how you should always be

You will never, never, never run out of good

Because the Lord God our father made good for free.

Important to Know

Psalm 100:5 NIV *"For the Lord is good and his mercy endures forever;"* God is good, and it is good to be good. Good generates good in a rather contagious way. Notice, when you do good other people start doing good. When people see other people doing good, they start doing good, and the cycle of doing good multiplies and continues the way God intended.

Example:

A group of students was heading to the cafeteria for lunch. As they walked, Tyra dropped some money on the floor. Two friends, Wanda and Alexus, saw Tyra drop the money and picked it up. Wanda wanted to keep the money. Alexus decided to give the money back. When Wanda saw Alexus give the money back, she decided to give the money back too.

Was it good that Wanda and Alexus gave Tyra back the money she dropped? Yes__ No__

It does not cost you anything to do good. True__ False__

Hitting

Hitting causes trouble and sometimes fights

Hitting is a form of bullying that is

Unacceptable and never right.

Important to Know

Proverbs 16:7 ESV *"When a man's ways please the Lord, he makes even his enemies to be at peace with him."* Nothing good comes from hitting someone. Hitting someone is an unacceptable assault that is against the law and your Student Code of Conduct. Hitting could cause negative reactions such as anger, fights, and violence, which carries consequences. So, think twice before you decide to hit someone.

Example:

There was a group of students sitting in a classroom. When the teacher stepped out, Zac dared fellow students to hit each other simply to post it on social media. Thomas accepted Zac's dare and hit Brandon, which started a fight. When the fight was over and recorded by several students, Thomas was arrested and suspended from school just because he wanted a few minutes of social media fame, which was not worth the trouble it caused him. The students who recorded the fight also got into trouble.

Are there consequences for hitting someone? Yes __   No __

Hitting someone could cause a fight. True __   False __

Greeting

Greet someone in the early morning

Greet someone in the mid-afternoon light

Greet someone in the cooler late evening sun

Greet your parents with a hug or kiss goodnight

Important to Know

I Corinthians 16:20 ESV *"All the brothers and sisters send you greetings. Greet one another with a holy kiss."* Greeting is sharing a friendly smile, asking, "how are you?" Saying, "good morning, good afternoon, good evening, goodnight, hi, hey, or hello." Greeting shows that you are friendly and polite. It puts positivity in the atmosphere and makes everyone feel friendly and refreshed. What better way to start a conversation and make new friends?

Example:

A substitute teacher was teaching a class. Unlike the regular teacher Ms. Thompson, the substitute teacher began the day by greeting the students. "Good morning, class," the substitute teacher said to the students. Her greeting the students made them feel good and welcome, which inspired them to listen, start greeting their parents, bus drivers, other teachers, and each other every day.

Do you think it is good to greet? Yes __ No __

Start greeting people and see what positive it brings.

Hurting Someone

Hurting someone causes injuries

Hurting someone causes emotional pain

Hurting someone in any way is an ungodly shame.

Important to Know

Ephesians 5:1, 2 NIV _"Follow God's example, therefore, as dearly loved children and walk in the way of love,"_ Hurting someone is not always a physical action. Mean and harsh words can hurt someone mentally, causing them to feel bad about themselves or emotionally by hurting their feelings. Sometimes hurting others is unintentional, but it becomes wrong when you purposely hurt someone.

Example:

   Two brothers, Roberto and Jose, were playing football on their video game. Jose starts laughing because his brother Roberto lost two games. Roberto became angry and punched Jose hurting him. Because Roberto hurt Jose, he was not allowed to play video games indefinitely.

   Arzelia and Meka laughed and made fun of Leslie, which hurt her feelings and caused her to feel bad about herself. As Leslie began to cry, they started making fun of her even more. Little did they know that Leslie was already hurting inside and needed a friend, kindness, and condolence because her mother had recently passed.

Roberto did not hurt Jose physically. True __   False __

Leslie was not hurt emotionally when Arzelia and Meka made fun of her. True __   False __

Helping Others

It's good to help others

Whenever there is a need

Helping others from your heart

Is what causes God to become pleased.

Important to Know

Matthew 5:16 KJV *"Let your light so shine before men, that they may see your good works, and glorify your Father which is in heaven."* Helping others shows Godly love, goodness, and kindness. It creates positive behavior; and makes the person you are helping feel happy. Helping others will also cause you to feel good about yourself because you made someone happy. When you help others, you are a blessing to those you help, and in turn, God blesses you.

Example:

Two siblings, Jarod and Macy, were having difficulty building a doghouse for their dog Lady. When their dad gave them a helping hand, building the doghouse was easier and more fun. Now Jarod and Macy know by experience how helping others can be a blessing and make a positive difference.

Kathy lived in a small home with her daughter Vanessa and son Alex. One day Kathy was cleaning up the house. Vanessa and Alex noticed and began helping her. It made her so happy that she ordered pizza when they finished.

Who helped Jarod and Macy? _____

Who made Kathy happy? _____

Judging Others

Everyone has an opinion

But not all opinions are true

Judge not others with your opinion

For you wouldn't want others to judge you.

Important to Know

Matthew 7:1, 2 NIV *"Do not judge, or you too will be judged. For in the same way you judge others, you will be judged,"* It is wise to judge one's character when someone seems suspicious. It is wise to use good judgment when choosing friends. But judging others by openly expressing your personal and negative thoughts, feelings or opinions is not good. Negative judgment creates gossip. Gossip breaks the peace and stirs up trouble because it usually lacks facts and truth. In that sense, if you don't have anything good to say about someone, it is better not to say anything.

Example:

Cindy and Pam began talking about Jean, a new girl in their classroom. They said, "Jean thinks she is better than they are because she does not like to sit in the back of the classroom with them and talk." The truth of the matter is, Jean sits in front of the classroom because she has poor hearing and vision.

It was okay for Cindy and Pam to judge Jean. True__   False __

If you do not have anything good to say about someone, it is better not to say anything. True __   False __

Integrity

Integrity is when you are always honest

Always fair and always tell the truth

It's when doing the right thing

Is what you always do.

Important to Know

I Corinthians 8:21 NIV *"For we are taking pains to do what is right, not only in the eyes of the Lord but also in the eyes of man."* Integrity is when you are honest, reliable, have moral principles and values. When you have integrity, you tell the truth, do what is good, fair, and right no matter what. Having integrity causes people to like and trust, which is good for your reputation.

Example:

Jonathon and Wendy wanted to go to the mall with their friends, but their mother didn't allow them to go because she didn't trust them. She didn't trust them because they have a reputation for being dishonest and not keeping their word. Now Wendy and Johnathan know by experience that your reputation will affect you in the long run.

Integrity is: Bad for your reputation __   Good for your reputation __

Underline or circle the words describing Integrity: Reliable, cheat, honest, trustworthy, dishonest, fair, lying, moral, unfair, good, righteous, bad, wrong, good reputation, immoral, moral values, moral principles, immoral values.

Kicking Someone

You should never ever kick anyone

Even if you're kicking for play

Kicking is so disrespectful

And could bring trouble

and fights your way.

Important to Know

Romans 13:10 NIV *"Love does no harm to a neighbor."* In the bible, the word (neighbor) is considered other people. Therefore, you should not harm another person, particularly by kicking them. Kicking is mean, cruel, and brutal. Kicking is an assault that causes injuries, provokes trouble, violence, and possible jail time.

Example:

Carl and Wang were scuffling on the ground after school. Carl's brother Lucious saw the scuffle and began kicking Wang until he was unconscious. Wang was taken to the hospital. All three students were suspended, but Lucious was suspended and taken to jail for kicking Wang.

Is kicking someone a bad thing to do? Yes__   No__

Which student got into the most trouble and why?

_____

_____

Keeping Your Word

Keeping your promise is most certainly a must

Your word is a promise, break that you break trust

Breaking trust with anyone is never a good thing to do

For when you don't keep your word people won't trust you.

Important to Know

I John 2:5 **NKJV** *"But whoever keeps His word, truly the love of God is perfected in him."* When you tell someone, you will do something; you are giving them your word. Your word is your bond (promise) and shouldn't be broken. Your reputation depends on keeping your word. When you don't keep your word, you appear to be a liar and are not trusted. Therefore, if you see that you cannot keep your word, let the person you gave your word know.

Example:

Mathis was always getting into fights during school. One day Mathis got into a fight and went to the principal's office. The principal was about to suspend Mathis until he gave his word that "he would not fight for the rest of the semester." The next semester the principal called Mathis into the office again but only to thank him for keeping his word. Now Mathis has a reputation for keeping his word rather than being a fighter.

When you can't keep your word, you should do what? Let the person know that you are not able to keep your word __ Say nothing __

Mathis did not keep his word to his principal. True __ False __

Killing

Thou shalt not kill

He that kills takes a life

A terrible deed that's never nice.

Important to Know

Exodus 20:13 NIV _"You shall not murder."_ Killing someone for a bad or unnecessary reason is wrong and one of the worse things anyone can do to another. Killing takes the life of the person who is killed forever. Killing a person takes that person away from their family and friends. Killing someone for reasons other than accidental or self-defense is against God's sixth commandment law and man's law of society. He who kills will have to face a judge in court and possibly be sentenced to life in prison. He will also have to face God one day for the life he purposely took.

Example:

Charles and Malisa robbed a man, then shot and killed him. They were on the run for over two weeks. Every knock on a door and every sound of a car spooked Charles and Malisa. They were barely able to get any sleep for fear of being captured. One morning about 4:00 am, the police did come to arrest Charles and Malisa as they so greatly feared but, instead of knocking at the door, they kicked the door down. Charles and Malisa were arrested and taken to jail.

The couple who killed the man was happy and slept well. True __ False__

There are no consequences for killing. True __ False __

Kindness

Kindness is to be friendly

To have love, be helpful and nice

To be compassionate and concerned

For others without having to think twice.

Important to Know

Proverbs 3:3 ICB _"Don't ever stop being kind and truthful. Let kindness and truth show in all you do."_ Let kindness show through your moral behavior by being nice, helpful, considerate, and caring of others. When you are kind, you will see that others will be kind. So, start being kind to others and see how much good your kindness will bring.

Example:

Virginia had just put together a hundred-piece puzzle during class and accidentally dropped it on the floor. All the students laughed except Sophia. Instead of laughing, Sophia began helping Virginia pick up pieces of the puzzle. Moments later, three other students began helping until all pieces were off the floor.

Joey had a dog on a chain. Keith, Joey's neighbor, saw that the dog wasn't happy on the chain, so he helped Joey put up a fence. When the fence was up, the dog was taken off the chain and happy.

Did Sophia's kindness inspire others to be kind too? Yes__ No__

It is good that Keith was kind to an animal. True__ False__

Littering

Littering defiles the earth

Littering is inconsiderate and wrong

So, don't be a litterbug respect the earth

Put your unwanted garbage where it belongs

Important to Know

Genesis 1:31 NIV *"God saw all that he had made and saw that it was very good."* Littering is wrong, unsightly, and against the law. Throwing candy wrappers, cups, cans, bottles, food, and other unwanted junk and garbage on the ground draws rats, roaches, flies, and other disease-carrying animals and insects. The germs and bacteria of litter can become a threat to everyone. Dogs, cats, and other animals get sick eating littered garbage. Littering stops up our sewers, causing streets to flood, pollutes our drinking water, rivers, and the ocean killing hundreds and thousands of fish, seals, turtles, and other marine animals. It is inconsiderate and somewhat rude to litter. It is also very costly to clean up.

Example:

Two siblings, Tisha and Kevin, were riding to the store with their parents. While on their way, they stopped for fast food and ordered lunch to go. When they arrived at the store, their parents gathered their bags, empty boxes, cups, and ketchup packages and threw them out of the car onto the ground before going into the store.

Was it okay for Tisha and Kevin's parents to litter since no one was around? Yes__ No__

If you wouldn't litter when a police officer is around, you shouldn't litter when a police officer is not around. Agree__ Disagree__

Listening

Listening will help you learn

Listening shows you have respect

Listening is when you pay close attention

And gain knowledge for whatever comes next.

Important to Know

James 1:19 BSB *"My beloved brothers, understand this: Everyone should be quick to listen, slow to speak, and slow to anger,"* It is good and polite to listen. Listening shows respect and that you are paying attention. People appreciate it when you listen and pay attention to them. Listening keeps you informed, focused, and calm. It also improves your attitude, patience, and ability to concentrate. Listening is a powerful skill to acquire.

Example:

The teacher was giving a homework assignment. Alex, Franklin, and Samantha were not listening. They did not have their homework assignment the following day because they were not listening and received failing marks.

James and Heather's mother were talking to them. Heather was back talking and not listening. James showed respect by being quiet, paying attention, and listening. By listening, James learned that his mother had purchased Netflix. However, Heather was not allowed to watch it.

How many students received failing marks by not listening? _____

Who was being disrespectful by not listening? James __ Heather __

Lying

Better to tell the truth

Than it is for you to tell a lie

Lying will only help a short while

For only a short while it may get you by

Important to Know

Proverbs 12:19 NIV *"Truthful lips endure forever, but a lying tongue lasts only a moment."* When you lie, you must remember the lie you told. There is nothing to remember when you don't lie because the truth never changes. Lying shows you are dishonest, lack integrity, and disrespect the person you are lying to, which could make them angry. You show respect when you tell the truth, and you're more likely to be forgiven. Lying makes matters worse.

Example:

   Phyllis and Gwen were cheating on their homework. When their mother asked if they cheated or not, Phyllis and Gwen said, "no." They didn't know that their mother saw them online cheating. In the end, she punished them one week for cheating and an additional two weeks for lying.

Why did Phyllis and Gwen get into trouble?

_____

_____

Did lying make matter worse for Phyllis and Gwen? Yes__   No__

Love

Love is beautiful and love is good

To love one another you always should

You should love everyone and God's animals too

Because God is the force of love and love we must do.

Important to Know

I Corinthians 13:4 NIV *"Love is patient, Love is kind. Love does not envy, it does not boast, it is not proud."* God is Love. Love is powerful, beautiful, and abundant. Everyone needs love. Love gives us a reason to live, be friendly, compassionate, save the lives of other people and animals. Love helps you feel good, experience joy and happiness. Showing love keeps the love of God flowing. So, show love for each other, animals, and nature and keep the love of God flowing.

Example:

Joseph asked his mother if she ever got tired of working? His mother replied, "yes." Joseph asked, "if she ever wishes she didn't have to pay out most of her money for bills?" His mother replied, "yes." "Then why do you continue doing it?" Joseph asked. "Because I love my family," she replied.

Why does Joseph's mother take care of him and his family? Because she loves them __ Because she doesn't love them __

Underline what is true: Draw a line through what is not true: Love is weak, love is powerful, it is godly to love, Satan is love, it's bad to love, it's good to love, you should love animals, love does not hate, you should not love animals, love is good, love makes you do bad things, loves makes you do good things.

Quitting School

You should never quit school

Neither should you ever drop out

Getting a good and decent education

Is what having a prospering future is about

Important to Know

Proverbs 18:15 ESV *"An intelligent heart acquires knowledge, and the ear of the wise seeks knowledge."* A good education can never be taken away from you. Education gives you the power to learn, knowledge to achieve, the ability to compete, succeed, and contribute to society. If you give up education, you give up the opportunity to learn and gain knowledge. Without knowledge, it is hard to grow and prosper. With competition for jobs being so competitive, a good education is essential to your future prosperity.

Example:

Roberto and Carlos are best friends. Carlos dropped out of school, Roberto stayed in school and graduated. He was able to get a good job, buy a beautiful home, a new car, and everything he needed. Carlos had trouble finding a job, and because he couldn't find a job, he had no place to live.

Who benefits from a good education? My parents__   My teacher__   Me__

A good education will help you to prosper in the future. True__   False__

Loyalty

He that is committed

Trustworthy faithful and true

Is considered loyal so, let that be you.

Important to Know

Proverbs 20:6 ISV *"Many claim I'm a loyal person! but who can find someone who truly is?"* Loyalty is when you are supportive, reliable, dedicated, and committed. When you take it upon yourself to be a true friend through the good and bad, you're a loyal friend. When you always look after your siblings, help bring in the groceries, be on time, and all such, you're loyal. When your parents take care of you, police protect and serve, citizens vote, or someone volunteers; they're loyal. Everybody needs somebody in some way or another, including animals. Without loyalty, you won't be able to depend on anyone.

Example:

Luke is dedicated to looking after his two siblings Gabriel and Abigail. He's also dedicated to feeding their dog Spike and keeping his room clean. His parents take good care of them and go to work every day to provide for them.

Is Luke loyal to his responsibilities? Yes__ No__

Luke's parents are loyal to him, his siblings, and their job. True__ False__

Robbery

You should never rob anyone at any time

Robbery is a bold, mean, bullying and selfish crime

Robbing someone can get you hurt or maybe even killed

Arrested by police and become an inmate where jails are filled.

Important to Know

Isaiah 61:8 NIV _"For I, the Lord, love justice; I hate robbery and wrongdoing."_ Taking from a person by force or intimidation is a form of robbery, which is against the law. Whether you choose to use a real weapon, a play weapon, or no weapon at all, the consequences of robbery or being with someone committing a robbery is jail time. Therefore, think before you act and choose your friends wisely.

Example:

Wesley and Jessie; wanted a new pair of sneakers but didn't have any money. So, they decided to rob a store using a toy gun that Jessie had. The store owner felt threatened and shot Jessie. The police caught Wesley and took him to jail. Wesley thought because he didn't have a weapon and his friend Jessie's weapon was a play gun, he would not have to go to jail. But Wesley did have to go to jail for thirty years because, during the robbery, his friend Jessie was killed.

Robbing is not serious if you use a toy gun. True___ False___

You could go to jail by being with someone committing a robbery. True___ False___

Making Peace

Peace is a calm friendly feeling

That you feel inside from deep within

It is good for you to make peace with others

Even more so with family or with an angry friend.

Important to Know

Romans 14:19 ESV "So then let us peruse what makes for peace and for mutual upbuilding." God favors people who make peace. Making peace is when you try to make things right by pointing out good and positive when tension or conflict occurs. Making peace is apologizing when there is anger or a grudge between you and someone else. It's making things better by doing and saying things that make people feel good, friendly, calm, and forgiving.

Example:

The teacher told Gina to choose two people to work on a project with her. Erica and Kelly were angry at each other so, Gina chose them in an effort to get them to work together and become friends. It worked. Gina did well making peace by bringing Erica and Kelly together. Now they're all friends.

God does not favor people who make peace. True__   False__

What did Gina do to make peace?

_____

_____

Selfish

When you want everything for yourself

Everything with no consideration

Neither care for anyone else

You're being quite selfish

And self-centered too.

Important to Know

Philippians 2:3 NIV *"Do nothing out of selfish ambition or vain conceit."* When you are inconsiderate, don't like to share, think only of yourself, want things to go your way even if it's unfair, you're selfish. To be in the likeness of God, you must possess godly qualities. Being selfish isn't a godly quality.

Example:

During a school picnic, Booley spilled his entire bag of potato chips. Jarvis was eating a large bag of potato chips and began laughing. When Jarvis finished eating the chips, there was some leftover. But rather than sharing his remaining chips, he threw the bag in the trash.

Being selfish is a godly quality. True __ False __

What do you think about Jarvis throwing the remaining chips in the trash?

_____

_____

Mercy

It's good to have mercy

For each other and friends

having a good heart to let go

Is where the power of mercy begins.

Important to Know

Matthew 5:7 NIV *"Blessed are the merciful for they shall obtain mercy."* To have mercy is to have kindness, pity, compassion, leniency, and forgiveness for someone who may or may not deserve it. It is to give someone another chance rather than hurt them or make matters worse for them.

Example:

Bruce was always teasing Timmy. One day Timmy saw Bruce alone and grabbed him by the front collar of his shirt. He was about to punch him until Bruce said, "I'm sorry for teasing you; I was only playing." Timmy hesitated for a moment and decided to let Bruce go.

Two friends, Perry and Quin, were together in a car. Quin began driving, drinking, and speeding. Perry wanted out, but Quin refused to stop and eventually crashed. Two weeks later, Perry died. Quin went to jail, but he asked Perry's parents to forgive him before he went, and they did.

Did Bruce have mercy on Timmy? Yes__ No__

Did Perry's parents have mercy on Quin? Yes__ No__

Smoking

Smoking isn't cool but rather its bad for your health

So, chose not to smoke and take good care of yourself.

Important to Know

I Corinthians 3:16 ESV _"Do you not know that you are God's temple and that God's spirit dwells in you?"_ Smoking is one way you can destroy your body. Smoking doesn't make you cool or give you swag. Smoking cigarettes, pipes, cigars-cigarillos, blunts, weed, vaping (e-cigarettes), or waterpipes are all bad for your health. Smoking also affects the health of others in the form of second-hand smoke. The chemical toxins in the things you smoke make smoking bad for your health.

Example:

Dennis, Rob, and Timbo were hanging out. Dennis and Rob start smoking. They tried to get Timbo to smoke by calling him a nerd and saying he was too scared to smoke, but Timbo was too smart to fall for it. By not smoking, Timbo proved he was in control of his own decisions and not easily influenced.

Did Timbo allow peer pressure to influence his decision not to smoke? Yes__ No__

Google and familiarize yourself with the toxins and negative effects of the following smoking items: Cigarettes, Cigars, Cigarillos, blunts, weed, vaping, and waterpipe.

Obedience

It is good to be obedient

And so disrespectful to disobey

You should always do as you're told

And respect authority figures every day.

Important to Know

I Peter 1:14 NLT _"So you must live as God's obedient children."_ Obedience is doing what you are asked to do, conducting yourself in an orderly manner by following rules, laws of society, and respecting authority. Obedience is also obeying your parents, teachers, principal, police officers and respecting your elders. When you are obedient, you will have more fun and freedom to do the things you enjoy doing. When you are disobedient, you enjoy less.

Example:

Paris and France, wanted to have a birthday party. When their mother asked them to clean their room, they didn't. Because of their disobedience, their mother didn't allow them to have the party they so badly wanted.

Carl and Victor, wanted to go to the movies with their friends Allen and Maurice. Carl and Victor's parents allowed them to go because their obedience has shown they have a sense of responsibility and can be trusted.

Disobedience did not work in Paris and France's favor. True__ False__

Obedience did not work out in Carl and Victor's favor. True__ False__

Spitting on Someone

Spitting on someone is nasty

Spitting on someone is very gross

Spitting on someone is disrespectful

Spitting on someone is a triple no, no, no.

Important to Know

Luke 6:31 CEV _"Treat others the way you want to be treated."_ Spitting on someone is very disrespectful. It sends a message that you think very little of the person you are spitting on. The act and disrespect of spitting on someone could get you into trouble with the law. Spitting on someone could also cause anger and rage, which could develop into fights and violence.

Example:

During school, Alex and Chang were arguing. Alex spat on Chang and caused him to become angry enough to fight. The principal viewed the school surveillance cameras and saw that Alex spit on Chang when the fight started. In the end, both students got into trouble but, since Alex spit on Chang, he was considered the aggressor and got into more serious trouble.

Is it okay to spit on someone? Yes ___ No ___

Can spitting on someone get you into trouble? Yes___ No___

How would you feel if someone spits on you? _____

Patience

It is good to be patient

Sometimes you must wait

So, learn to wait and be patient

For self-control and goodness sake.

Important to Know

Galatians 5:22 ESV *"But the fruit of the Spirit is love, joy, peace, patience, kindness, goodness, faithfulness, gentleness, self-control;"* Being patient helps you to be obedient and disciplined. Being patient also helps you accept waiting without developing an attitude, getting angry, or becoming frustrated. When you are patient, you are calm and have self-control. When you are not patient, you tend to lack self-control, rush, become selfish, frustrated, and angry.

Example:

    Three students, Trecia, Becky, and Lauri needed to cross a busy street. Trecia was patient and waited for the light to change to red before crossing the street. Becky and Lauri were not patient, so they ran across the busy street while the light was green. Becky barely made it across the street. Sadly, Lauri was hit by a car. Trecia was never at risk of being hit by a car because she was patient.

Who was hit by the car by not being patient?

_____

Being patient helps you to accept having to wait. True__ False__

Stealing

Thou shalt not steal

For stealing is a crime

Stealing is breaking the law

Which the penalty is jail time.

Important to Know

Exodus 20:15 KJV *"God's Eight Commandment. Thou shalt not steal."* Stealing is wrong and unacceptable. When you steal, you are taking from someone and breaking the law. When you break the law, you risk getting into trouble and going to jail. If a background check is needed one day for a job, your record will show that you were once a thief and likely cannot be trusted.

Example:

After school, Justice put his cell phone and wallet in his book bag so he could play basketball. A bystander was caught on video stealing Justice's cell phone and wallet out of his bookbag. The bystander was arrested and taken to a juvenile detention center.

Was stealing the cell phone and wallet worth the bystander getting into trouble and going to juvenile? Yes ___ No ___

Is stealing against God's Ten Commandment laws? Yes___ No___

How would you feel if someone stole something from you?

_____

_____

Respect

Self-respect is good

Respecting others is too

Having respect for one another

Is always a good and moral thing to do.

Important to Know

I Peter 2:17 NIV _"Show proper respect to everyone, love the family of believers, fear God, honor the emperor."_ Respect is when you recognize someone you feel deserves to be treated kindly, special, and with courtesy. You should always respect yourself and others. You show respect by treating people the way you want to be treated. You show self-respect by how you talk, wear your clothes, carry yourself, maintain self-control, and by the decisions you make.

Example:

A group of students was standing at a bus stop. Girls were allowing boys to touch them inappropriately as they yelled and cursed in the presence of an adult woman. Kwame, a fellow student, asked them to stop, but their behavior got worse. The following week Madison, one of the students whose behavior was disrespectful at the bus stop, went on a job interview. She did not get the job because the interviewer was the lady standing at the bus stop on the day Madison and her friends behaved disrespectfully.

You should always respect others and your <u>s</u> __ __ f.

Cursing, yelling, and inappropriate touching in public are okay if no one sees you. True__ False__

Taking

Taking can get you arrested

Taking could cause a fight

It's a form of bullying

That's never right.

Important to Know

James 4:17 ESV *"So whosoever knows the right thing to do and fails to do it, to him it is sin."* Taking is wrong no matter the size or value of the item one decides to take. Taking small things leads to taking bigger things. It doesn't matter if you're home, at school, or in public. Taking is a form of robbery that is against the law and will not be tolerated.

Example:

Two bullies, Bobby and Drew, took Phillip's cellphone and refused to give it back. When Phillip informed the principal, Bobby and Drew were suspended from school and warned they would be arrested if it happened again.

Margaret took Serena's ink pen. Because it was only an ink pen, Margaret thought she would not get into trouble for taking it, but she did. The principal warned Margaret if it happened again, she would be suspended.

Bobby and Drew were wrong for taking Phillip's cellphone? True__ False__

It's okay to take something from someone if it's small. True __ False __

Right and Wrong

You can never ever go wrong by doing what is right

Know that God sees everything beneath the sun so bright.

Important to know

II Corinthians 5:10 KJV *"For we must all appear before the judgement seat of Christ; that everyone may receive the things done in his body, according to that he hath done, whether it be good or bad."* What is right is good and always will be good. What is wrong is bad and always will be bad. Right is right, and wrong is wrong whether anyone sees you do it or not. Know that God sees you and rewards you accordingly. **Hebrew 4:13 NIV** *"Nothing in all creation is hidden from God's sight."*

Example:

Author lost his school ID. Jordan found it and mailed it to Author's address. No one saw Jordan mail Author's ID, but God did. A month later, Jordan was surprised with one hundred dollars for his birthday; what an awesome blessing to reap by doing right.

Larry stole a laptop from school, but no one saw him steal it. He took the laptop home but couldn't use it because it had a virus. No one ever knew Larry stole the laptop, but God knew it. Three months later, someone broke into Larry's home and stole his electronics. What a terrible consequence to reap by doing wrong.

When you do right, God will bless you whether anyone sees you do good or not. True__ False___

When you do wrong, God will allow you to reap bad whether anyone sees you do bad or not. True__ False__

Talking About Others (Gossiping)

Talking and chatting among others

Is an activity we participate from day to day

But spreading rumors is considered gossip by the way

Important to know

Proverbs 16:28 NIV *"A perverse person stirs up conflict, and a gossiper separates close friends."* Gossip is bad-mouthing, spreading rumors, and talking about someone's personal or private business. Gossiping also says things that are not true and lack facts for no good reason. Not all gossip is bad gossip. But when you talk about someone negatively because you don't like them, are jealous of them, or envy them, you are gossiping in a bad way. Although gossiping shares news, it is never good to secretly gossip natively about anyone. When you gossip, people always add their negative version to what you have said when they share your gossip, which results in conflict, anger, and sometimes violence.

Example:

Sadie, Gigi, and Sandy are friends. When Gigi left, Sadie started gossiping about her to Sandy. Sandy listened but didn't agree or comment about anything Sadie said about Gigi. Sandy didn't get involved with negative gossip because she knew it was wrong and would have affected her friendship with Gigi.

Write the name of the person who started gossiping.

_____

Negative gossip is okay if no one finds out what you said. True__ False__

Sacrifice

It's good when you decide to sacrifice for someone

Without considering yourself through your efforts and time

To make a difference in the life of someone with a heart to be kind.

Important to Know

Ephesians 5:2 CEV *"Let love be your guide. Christ loved us and offered his life for us as a sacrifice that pleases God."* To sacrifice is to consider the need or desire of another person over your own. Sacrificing is giving your time by visiting someone, helping someone, giving up something of value to you, such as clothes, shoes, games, and other things that will make a difference in someone else's life.

Example:

Two brothers, James and Steve, bought Six Flags tickets along with a few friends. James became sick and was unable to go. Rather than go to Six Flags without James, Steve sacrificed his opportunity by giving his tickets away and staying home with his brother.

There was a fire in a housing complex. Several people were left homeless. One of the fire victims was Chance, a student. Chance's friends Orlando and Rodney created a GoFundMe page and raised five thousand dollars for the fire victims. They also started a clothing drive and sacrificed their time collecting clothes, shoes, and furniture for the fire victims.

Who sacrificed in the first story? _____

Who sacrificed their time for the fire victims in the second story?

_____

Teasing

Making fun of someone by teasing

Can make one feel embarrassed and sad

Teasing to make fun can also make one feel bad

Teasing can be a bad experience for someone who is new

Teasing just to make someone feel bad is not a nice thing to do.

Important to know

Ephesians 5:4 ESV _"Let there be no filthiness nor foolish talk nor crude joking, which are out of place, but instead let there be thanksgiving."_ Teasing can be fun when two or more people are teasing each other. But teasing someone who doesn't want to be teased or just to make fun of them is wrong. Unwanted teasing can be emotionally hurtful and viewed as being bullied, picked on, or harassed. Unwanted teasing can also lead to anger, revenge, and violence.

Example:

Edward and Julius were teasing Chad during class, which made him feel bad. He told them he didn't think their teasing was funny, but they continued teasing him. The next day Chad was about to respond to their teasing through violence but was stopped before he could do anything.

It is okay to tease someone who does not want to be teased. True___ False___

Can teasing lead to violence? Yes___   No___

Serving

Jesus lived his life

Doing good by serving others

A moral example we all shall follow

And practice always as sisters and brothers.

Important to Know

Mark 10:43 NIV *"Instead whoever wants to become great among you must be your servant,"* A servant is a person who serves others (do for others). It is easy to serve. When Jesus was on earth, He spent much of his life serving others. You do not have to be perfect, special, or an A student to serve. You do not have to be popular, rich, have fancy clothes, shoes, or cars to serve. To serve, all you need is a heart of love and a desire to help make a positive difference in the lives of others. When you serve, God considers you a great person.

Example:

Two friends, Bobby and Josh, were known for serving others. They always volunteered when they saw a need, whether home or away from home. Bobby and Josh served by visiting the sick and elderly, donating clothes, shoes, and other items people needed to make a positive difference in their life.

Write one or two things Bobby and Josh did to serve. _____
_____

Think of what you can do to serve your parents or someone else and do it.

Two Wrongs Don't Make It Right

If someone does you wrong

It's not good to do them wrong too

Keep the peace stay away if you might

Because doing wrong too won't make it right.

Important to Know

Roman 12:17 NIV _"Do not repay anyone evil for evil."_ When someone does you wrong, it is not good to seek revenge. If you do wrong because someone else does wrong, you become equally wrong as them. When everybody is doing wrong, who will represent good and stand up for what is right?

Example:

Jada and Susan were spreading rumors on social media about Jamie, a new girl at school. Jamie's friend Makiah said to her, "since Jada and Susan spread rumors about you, you should spread rumors about them too." Jamie refused her friend's suggestion because her mother taught her that two wrongs don't make it right nor better. Jamie decided the moral thing to do was to ignore the rumors.

Jamie's decision to ignore the rumors was a good decision. True__

 False__

What did Jamie's mother teach her?

_____

_____

Sharing

Sharing expresses care and love

It makes a big difference to others

And most certainly pleases God above.

Important to Know

Hebrews 13:16 ESV *"Do not neglect to do good and to share what you have, for such sacrifices are pleasing to God."* Sharing is a form of giving or sacrificing a part of what you have so that others may have too. Sharing creates a positive attitude, friendship, and happiness. It also motivates others to share.

Example:

Mia, Alana, and Kim were about to watch a movie. Mia's mother gave each of the three girls a large bowl of popcorn and a soda of their choice. Alana dropped her popcorn on the floor. After the girls cleaned up the popcorn, Mia shared her popcorn with Alana. When Kim saw Mia sharing her popcorn, she began sharing too. All three girls enjoyed popcorn, soda, and a movie simply because Mia and Kim shared.

What is good about the above story?

_____

_____

Do you like popcorn? Yes__   No__

What is your favorite soda? _____

Touching Inappropriately

When you hear no to touching

Touching Is inappropriate for you to do

Whenever you touch someone inappropriately

Best believe that trouble will be waiting ahead for you

Important to Know

Ephesians 5:11 ESV "*Take no part in the unfruitful works of darkness, but instead expose them.*" You should never touch anyone who does not want to be touched, even more so inappropriately. There is a difference between play touching and inappropriate touching. Inappropriate touching could get you into serious trouble. Your parents can explain to you what inappropriate touching is.

Example:

Tracy was visiting her Aunt Betty and Uncle Buck. When Tracy was alone with Uncle Buck, he touched her inappropriately. Tracy told her mother what Uncle Buck had done, and Uncle Buck got into serious trouble with the law.

During class, Chan touched Kate inappropriately. Kate asked Chan to stop, but he didn't. Kate told her teacher what Chan had done. Chan was suspended from school and warned he could get into serious trouble if he touched anyone inappropriately again.

When someone says no or stop, you should stop even if you think they don't truly mean it? True___   False___

It is okay to tell someone if a relative touch you inappropriately. True_ False___

Smile

He that shares a smile

Brings joy cheer and gleam

But he that mopes around and frowns

Bitters the atmosphere when he's around

Important to Know

Proverbs 17:22 ESV *"A joyful heart is good medicine, but a crushed spirit dries up the bones."* It's good to smile. Smiling brings joy and sends a positive message that you are friendly and are in a good mood. Smiling can make someone who is feeling sad or angry feel happy. Smiling is contagious because when you smile, others smile too.

Example:

Twins, Addie and Mattie, attend the same school. On their first day, they felt uncomfortable because they didn't know anyone. When they entered their classroom for the first time, some students said nothing, and some smiled. Addie and Mattie no longer felt uncomfortable because they knew that some of the students were friendly when they smiled.

Which word describes what is better for you to do? Smile__   Frown__

How do you feel when someone smiles at you? Good __   Bad __

Threatening Someone

It's illegal to threaten someone

By boasting harm you are going to do

It doesn't matter if you're a male or female

Threating is illegal and will cause trouble for you.

Important to Know

Rom 12:18 ESV *"If possible, so far as it depends on you, live peaceably with all."* Anytime you post online, call, or tell someone you are going to harm or hurt them in any way is considered a threat. It doesn't matter if you are playing or serious; threatening someone in any way is a crime and carries serious consequences.

Example

Winston decided to play a prank by posting online that he would be bringing a weapon to school and hurt everybody he didn't like. When Winston arrived at school the next day, the police were waiting for him. Although Winston had no weapon, he was taken to jail anyway for making terroristic threats. Now Winston has a police record.

You will not get into trouble if you threaten someone online. True__ False__

It is not good or lawful to make threats. True__ False__

Thank You

When someone gives you something

Or when someone does something nice for you

Saying thank you is courteous and the right thing to do.

Important to Know

I Thessalonians 5:18 KJV _"In everything give thanks, for this is the will of God in Christ Jesus concerning you."_ It is good to say, "thank you." Saying "thank you" shows you are grateful and appreciate when someone has given you something, helped you, or complimented you. Saying thank you also shows courtesy, respect, and acknowledgment. When you say thank you, people notice your good manners and appreciate you more.

Saying "thank you" also includes giving thanks to God for everything when you pray and for the food you eat when you say, your grace.

Example:

Calita and Andria happen to drop their books on the floor at the same time. Orlando helped them pick up their books. Adria said, "thank you," but Calita said nothing.

Which one of the two students expressed their appreciation?

_____

You should give God thanks for everything when you pray and thank God for your food before you eat by saying your grace. True ___   False ___

Violence

Violence causes more trouble

Than it could ever possibly solve

The more you decide to participate

The more deeply you become involved

Important to Know

Psalm 11:5 NIV *"The Lord examines the righteous, but the wicked, those who love violence, he hates with a passion."* Violence is never the right answer to solving a problem. Violence is against the law and is not worth the trouble it gets you into. Violence affects many people, including people who are not involved. No one wants to go to jail or die by violence so, do the right thing and live a No-Beef nonviolent life.

Example:

Camia, Jenny, and Vivian were arguing. Camia noticed Jenny and Vivian were getting angry, so she decided to stop arguing and walked away. Jenny and Vivian continued arguing and began fighting. Jenny picked up a rock and hit Vivian, injuring her. Although both Jenny and Vivian got into trouble for fighting, Jenny was also arrested for using a rock as a weapon to hurt Vivian.

Walking away can help you avoid violence. True___ False___

Using a weapon makes matters worse. True___ False___

Violence solves problems. True___ False___

Treat Others the Way You Want to Be Treated

Everyone wants to be treated with love and respect

Since you truly like to be treated with love and respect too

Then treating others with love and respect is what you must do.

Important to Know

Luke 6:31 ESV "And as you wish that others would do to you, do so to them." Treating others the way you want to be treated is the (moral way) God's way of making sure that everyone is treated equally with love, goodness, kindness, and respect. Treating others the way you want to be treated is easy. All you must do is treat others the way you would like to be treated.

Example:

Maxine, a student known for being mean, fell and dropped her lunch tray on the cafeteria floor. Everybody was laughing except Faith, a girl who practices good morals. Faith walked over to Maxine, helped her up, and asked if she was okay. It made Maxine feel better and respond with a positive attitude. Faith's best friend Brenda asked her, "why did you help Maxine when she fell and dropped her tray?" Faith replied, "because that's how I would like to be treated if it were me."

You should always treat others the way you want to be treated. True __ False __

Treating others the way you want to be treated is the moral way. True__ False__

Racism

Why dislike someone because they're

Different or because of the color of their skin

God wants us to always love each other like sisters

And brothers and live in harmony together as friends

If you should ever meet someone that's different than you

Do be friendly and accept them because God created them too.

Important to Know

Malachi 2:10 KJV _"Have we not all one father? Hath not one God created us?"_ We are all brothers and sisters in the eyes of God. It was God's creative choice to make people different. Disliking someone because of their race or skin color is racist. God created different races for his own reason, just as he created the four seasons, spring, summer, autumn, and winter, to be different. God created different animals, trees, and plants too. How do you think it would be if everyone looked the same or just like you?

Example:

Kashima and Ricardo are different races. They wanted to be friends with all the students in class, but two didn't like them because of their race. When the other students accepted Kashima and Ricardo, the two students who didn't accept them before realized that color and race don't matter when making new friends, so they accepted them too.

All races are equal. True___   False___

No race is superior to another. True___   False___

Trustworthy

The qualities of integrity and truth

Are qualities that cause people to trust you.

Important to Know

Proverbs 10:9 GWT *"Whoever lives honestly will live securely, but whoever lives dishonestly will be found out."* He that is trustworthy is always honest and keeps his word (his promise). He that is trustworthy doesn't take nor steal whether anyone is around or not. Being trustworthy reflects your reputation. It also makes you valuable and special in a way that when people hear your name, they hear the name of a person they can trust and depend on.

Example:

Drew, a middle school student, wanted to stay home alone while his mother attended a birthday party. But, since Drew was always viewing websites, he knew he shouldn't be, lying about his homework and school conduct, his mother doesn't trust him. She doesn't trust him because she believes he may do something foolish and lie about it. She said to him, "if you would be more honest and obedient, maybe one day, I will allow you to stay home alone. But, if you don't, you will need a sitter or must stay with a relative whenever I'm away from home, no matter how old you are.

People trust you when you are trustworthy. True__ False__

How can Drew gain his mother's trust?

_____

_____

Revenge

Vengeances is mine

Are the words of Almighty God

He that has a desire to seek revenge

Lacks the forgiveness of God in his heart

Important to Know

Roman 12:19 ESV "_Beloved, never avenge yourselves, but leave it to the wrath of God, for it is written, Vengeance is mine, I will repay says the Lord._" Revenge is when you choose to get back at someone. To hurt or harm someone who may in some way or another have hurt or harmed you, someone you love or care for. Revenge is not a good thing to pursue nor have in your heart. Revenge never solves anything but rather makes matters worse by promoting hate, bitterness, hostility, further revenge, or violence. Revenge also may hinder you from forgiving and moving forward with peace of mind.

Example:

Two students, Rico and Richard, beat up Derick, a fellow student. When Derick's friends learned of his beating, they were angry and wanted revenge. Derick knew that getting revenge would only create further violence, so instead, he reported Rico and Richard to the proper authorities, and they got into trouble.

Revenge could cause violence. True__ False__

Seeking revenge could hinder you from forgiving. True__ False__

Understanding

Always try to be understanding

Whenever things cannot go your way

Because things will not always go in your favor

Sometimes you'll have to adjust to have a better day

Important to Know

Proverbs 3:5 NIV *"Trust in the Lord with all your heart and lean not to your own understanding."* To be understanding, you must be attentive, have a positive attitude, be open-minded, thoughtful, and able to picture yourself in someone else's situation. Not everything that happens in life will seem fair or make sense. Understanding will help you accept and adjust to those things that do not seem fair or make sense in life.

Example:

Christine, a mother, promises to take Nancy and Angela to the State Fair the upcoming weekend. When the weekend arrived, she explained to them that she unexpectantly had to work and would take them the following weekend. When that weekend arrived, she explained that she was too tired to take them. Nancy became angry, but Angela didn't. Eventually, Christine was able to take them to the Fair. She also surprised Angela with a new pair of sneakers for being understanding.

It is good to be understanding of people and situations. True___ False___

Which sibling got a new pair of sneakers and why?

_____

_____

Rude

Rude is having bad manners and being impolite

It's an inconsiderate behavior that is never good or right

Being rude is when you're jumping a line no matter who's next

With a selfish habit of having your way through means of disrespect.

Important to Know

I Corinthians 14:40 KJV "*Let all things be done decently and in order.*"
Being rude is discourteous and shows you have a bad attitude and lack
manners. It's bumping into someone without saying, "excuse me," being
bold and unpleasant to others without care or consideration of what is
right or wrong simply to have your way at all costs. There is no order or
respect when one is rude. Being rude leads to further rudeness, anger, and
sometimes violence.

Example:

A group of students lined up to receive a free brand-new pair of
wireless earbuds. After half the students received free earbuds, the supply
ran short. When Romeo was about to receive the last pair, Simon jumped
the line and grabbed them. The teacher took the earbuds away from
Simon and gave them to Romeo. Simon's rude behavior caused him to be
disqualified and unable to return to receive free earbuds the following
day.

Simon's behavior was not rude. True___ False___

It is okay to be rude sometimes. True___ False___

When to Wait

When someone is exiting

It is polite and courteous to wait

For them to pass first for goodness sake.

Important to Know

Ephesians 4:2 NLT *"Always be humble and gentle. Be patient with each other,"* When you are about to enter a bus or building of any sort, if someone is about to exit, the polite thing to do is wait until they exit or pass first before you to enter. Waiting shows you are selfless, courteous, and considerate, which are good moral qualities.

Example:

A group of students was exiting a building while another group of students was waiting to enter the same building. Suddenly the students who were waiting began entering the building while the students were exiting the building, which caused conflict.

Which group of students should have waited?

The students who were exiting the building. __

The students who were waiting to enter the building. __

It is good and polite to allow someone to exit before you enter. Ture__ False__

Vandalism

Vandalism is a bad and immature behavior

That leaves private and public property wrecked

A deliberate act of reckless destruction and disrespect.

Important to know

Proverbs 25:28 NLT *"A person without self-control is like a city with broken-down walls."* Vandalizing is deliberately destroying, crashing, breaking, drawing, and spraying (graffiti) on public or private property for fun (pranks) or worse (hate). People who vandalize lacks self-control, care, consideration, and respect for people and the community. Things damaged or destroyed by vandalism are expensive to repair or replace; some are irreplaceable. Vandalism is a crime that is taken very seriously.

Example:

Mickey, Corey, and Alvin were observed spraying the gold posts and destroying lines and numbers on a newly marked football field. They got into serious trouble with the law and lost their college scholarships.

Hector, Wang, Adrian, and Deangelo drove through a neighborhood running over mailboxes, egging homes, spray painting doors, cars, and throwing rolls of toilet paper through tree branches just for fun.

It is wrong to vandalize. True__ False__

Vandalizing is serious, costly, and against the law. True__ False__

Yes Ma'am – Yes Sir

You shouldn't respond to adults

The way you would each other or friends

Simply saying Yes ma'am and yes sir to adults

Is not necessarily wrong or right it's simply polite.

Important to Know

Proverbs 25:11 NASB *"Like apples of gold in settings of silver, is a word spoken at the proper time."* It is good and polite to say yes ma'am to adult women and yes sir to adult men. Saying yes ma'am and yes sir shows courtesy and respect to your elders and recognition of authority. A good way to start saying "yes ma'am and "yes sir" is by practicing saying it to your parents and teachers.

Example:

   A teacher sent Kathy and Frankie to the principal's office for using profanity (cursing) in the classroom. The principal asked each of the students if they used profanity in the classroom or not. Kathy replied saying, "yeah." Frankie replied saying, "yes sir."

Which of the two students showed respect towards the authority figure? Kathy __ Frankie __

It is polite to say "yes ma'am and "yes Sir" to your elders (adults) and authority figures. True __   False __

I hope you have enjoyed this book and learned some good life lessons. If you want to get the most out of this book or any book, it is good to reread it because there are certain things you may not quite catch or understand until the second or third time around.

If you like what you read, share your newly gained wisdom and knowledge of this book with family and friends.

Final Thoughts:

About the Author

Darryl Barron is a southerner raised in the Peach State of Georgia. Darryl Barron has experience in Motivational Speaking and Life Coaching. He also has a love for children, working with them and instilling within them good morals. He has two other books published, entitled The 3 Elements Of Love (a relationship book) and Victory Over Sorrow. He has also written books that have yet to be published entitled How Not to Worry About Anything, Short Story Twists, and several children's stories.

Made in the USA
Columbia, SC
15 June 2023

18131555R00072